Market Capitalism and Christianity

Market Capitalism
and Christianity

Jim Halteman

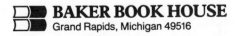

BAKER BOOK HOUSE
Grand Rapids, Michigan 49516

Printed in the United States of America

Library of Congress Cataloging-in-Publication Data

Halteman, Jim.
    Market capitalism and Christianity.

    Bibliography: p.
    Includes index.
    1. Capitalism—Religious aspects—Chris-
tianity. 2. Capitalism—Religious aspects
—Anabaptists. 3. Anabaptists—Doctrines.
I. Title.
BR115.C3H36   1989   261.8'5   88-7728
ISBN 0-8010-4327-1

To my mother and father,
Wilmer and Perle Halteman,
who never preached stewardship;
they just practiced it.

Contents

	Foreword	9
	Preface	11
	Introduction	13
1	The Economic Context	17
2	Allocation of Resources	22
3	Biblical Background to Economic Thinking	35
4	The Two-Kingdom Approach to the Bible	43
5	Reading the Bible with Modern Glasses	54
6	A Radical Economic Model for Today	65
7	The Model Illustrated	88
8	Individual Freedom and Private Property: The First Pillar	101
9	The Harmony of Self-Interested Behavior: The Second Pillar	109
10	Limited Government Activity: The Third Pillar	119
11	From Models to Reality	138
12	Being in the World But Not of It	145
	Glossary	163
	Suggested Readings	171
	Subject Index	173
	Scripture Index	176

Foreword

Economics strikes many people as the "dismal science." Widely read Christian literature on economics strikes me as contentious. This book is neither dismal nor contentious. It is not "lite" or sappy either. It is judicious without being dull. It is provocative without being polemic. Nor is it just for Christian readers.

Beginning students of economics will here see economics with a human face. Those who go on into business will be persuaded against the defeatism that says "the market made me do it." I hope that overly optimistic entrepreneurs and budding social reformers will be sobered and instructed by the constraining economic forces that are described cogently. I also hope that pamphleteers and sloganeers of all stripes will cease fire long enough to consider this book a beginning to the destruction of the "dividing walls of hostility."

The author's aim is to introduce both the market system and the place of Christian discipleship within it. In introducing the market system, he is careful (unlike most economists) to reveal the foundational role of ethics, social instincts, and institutions such as family, firm, court, and church. In discussing market discipleship, he is careful (unlike most Christians) *not* to claim that this is a settled matter. He describes many of the important alternative views of market discipleship, and he reasons from one of them. His view favors a special place for the community of believers as a locus for economic reform, relief, discipline, decision making, and perhaps even experimentation.

The author is both a professional economist and a practicing disciple. Thus this book is no untested ivory-tower treatise, no utopian grand plan. The reader should appreciate that the author has been experimenting for years with exactly the market discipleship that he outlines, and all the while observing the experiment as a social scientist. His writing is practical, personal, and professing. But it is professional, too. There are no woolly compromises with the economic way of thinking. There are no implicit, awkward apologies for having fallen in early life into the waywardness of economics. There are no wistful, amateurish attempts at theology or ethics.

There are admitted gaps in the treatment, but they are, in my opinion, wise. The author's focus is microeconomics. He says little about macro- or international economics. These areas—the economics of stabilization and of competing sovereignties—are distinctively thorny and complex. So is the issue of ideal economic relationship between states defined by boundaries and a church that ought to know none. I am eager for believing economists to write at least two more books to fill these gaps. May they be as probing, fervent, and practical as this one.

J. David Richardson
Department of Economics
University of Wisconsin–Madison

Preface

The preface to this book is chapter 7. In that chapter I reflect upon the influences that led to these thoughts. There is no way to sort out the most important contributors. Perhaps it was the volunteer from church who helped in the harvest on our farm thirty-five years ago, or the theologians who critiqued the middle chapters. The final product profited significantly from the careful critique and timely suggestions of P. J. Hill and J. David Richardson. My colleagues in the Business and Economics Department at Wheaton College willingly participated in numerous discussions of the manuscript content. My wife and children, along with my church and small group, have often, unknowingly, called me back from the urge to preach in this book. Some will say they failed, but if the message of a discipling process dominates over pat answers, they deserve considerable credit. Where I rejected or altered the advice of others or improperly researched the content, I am solely responsible and I welcome the reader's critique.

First Corinthians 13 has become a favorite passage of mine, not because of the beautiful poetic content that shows the dynamics of a successful community of faith, but rather because of verse 12. "Now we see but a poor reflection . . . ; then we shall see face to face. Now I know in part; then I shall know fully, even as I am fully known." This effort to focus the poor reflection a bit more sharply can never result in a perfect image but it can, I hope, stimulate thinking toward a clearer view of these important matters.

Introduction

My standard of living is no one's business but my own."

"The Bible teaches against accumulated wealth."

"Market capitalism is the only economic system a Christian should support."

"Scriptural teaching on economic matters is directed toward an agricultural no-growth environment and therefore is not very relevant today."

"The Christian's primary task is to infiltrate the economic structures of the world to win them for Christ."

Over the years these statements, or variations of them, have surfaced again and again in many settings. Simple responses to them have never seemed adequate. Discussions of these statements invariably lead to theological and economic issues that create endless debate. Thus my attempt to deal with these and other issues relating to the Christian faith and market capitalism is not without some risk. I hope that throughout the book the challenges to faithful stewardship will come through in a helpful way.

My training as an economist and my study of biblical and theological material represent only part of the background material for this book. Perhaps the most compelling source has been my experience in the community of faith at various places. Over the last several decades I have come to believe that the desire for self-sufficiency and autonomy is a stumbling block for believers. My most inspiring challenge has been to help build the church at the levels of congregation, conference, and denomination. I am more

13

convinced now than ever that the economics of the Bible can best be understood in the context of a community of faith. Both the Old Testament and the New seem to proclaim that message from beginning to end.

At the same time I am not optimistic that any secular economic system can provide true economic well-being. Market capitalism can deliver goods and services in amazing quantities, but it cannot guarantee caring communities that sustain body and spirit. In fact, despair and loneliness lurk amid the plenty, and competitive capitalism has not been able to erase them. The Christian faith offers an answer to this despair, but Christian people need a strategy that will help them to be true to Scripture and to be responsible stewards of resources. This book suggests such a strategy.

There are two agendas for the Christian to pursue. First, the believer should attempt to help the church design and practice the kind of economic behavior that will witness to the emerging kingdom of God. This witness is not a utopian dream, but an exciting possibility for all believers. It can also be a powerful—though largely untapped—tool of evangelism.

Second, the believer needs to understand and affect the secular capitalistic system of which western Christians are a part. This involves the difficult task of connecting two ideologies that have limited compatibility. In other words, the community of faith must practice biblical values together while it interacts in a secular world that has different goals.

The tension believers experience between the two agendas is depicted by this continuum:

practicing values of the kingdom of God (modelers)	influencing values of the secular system (infiltrators)

Modelers, as they are called here, believe that Christians have a special calling to practice values not common in a secular world. They believe that being in the world but not of the world has specific implications for life. Infiltrators, in contrast, see the Christian task primarily as infiltrating the structures of society to influence people and social institutions for good.

Infiltrators criticize modelers, believing they are too uninvolved in social structures. They believe that modelers' efforts to live out the teachings of the kingdom of God in the real world are utopian and lead to an ineffective outward ministry. In contrast, modelers see infiltrators as compromisers who sell out to the world. They argue that infiltrators have lost the radical calling of the gospel and have adopted the world's standards of success and power.

Obviously I have described the extremes of the continuum. In reality, most believers live between the extremes. However, it is a thesis of this book that believers today have moved too far to the infiltrator side of the continuum and need to feel a tug back toward the modeling side. There will always be tension pulling a believer from both sides of the continuum as long as we "see through a glass darkly," but there are times when circumstances make us more susceptible to err on one side or the other. The pluralistic, tolerant society in which we live, the material well-being that many believers enjoy, and the moral relativism of our time have made infiltration the easy alternative in the latter half of the twentieth century in much of the capitalistic western world.

This book has four related parts. First, it discusses the essentials of any economic system. No matter what the economic system in view, the tasks of allocation and production must be organized in some fashion consistent with the values and social patterns of society. We must understand this background of what economics is all about before we can be prepared to consider any specific methods of economic organization for either the kingdom of God or the secular world.

Second, the book sketches the kind of economic relationships a modeler might propose for the community of believers and presents some simple hermeneutical and theological considerations to set the stage for the model.

Third, the book considers the economic world that western Christians are attempting to infiltrate. It explores three pillars of market capitalism in order to understand the differences between values of the kingdom of God and values of the secular institutions of western market economies.

Finally, the book suggests ways for the community of faith to interact effectively with market capitalism without selling out to its spirit. To model without becoming isolated and to infiltrate without selling out to the world are the ideals to which this book points.

Two groups of people will benefit most from this book. The first consists of students beginning the study of economics. The part on market capitalism will help to give an intuitive sense of what economics is all about and how capitalism solves economic problems. The part that sketches the economics of the believer's church will challenge the student to evaluate economic behavior in light of biblical content. The conclusions are controversial and should foster constructive debate. The discussion questions at the end of each chapter help to focus the issues involved in each topic.

The second audience consists of people involved in policy issues from a biblical perspective who have little economic training. The perspective on market capitalism presented here should be useful for ministers and laypeople alike who seek viewpoints on various economic concerns.

This book represents the Anabaptist approach to Christian practice. The two-kingdom model developed in chapter 4 contrasts with the alternate view that any Christian model must be generally applicable to believers and nonbelievers alike because all of creation must be subject to the moral will of the same Creator. Anabaptist thought has always had radical counterculture threads that challenge the believer to a life of discipleship that does not make sense to unbelievers. This counterculture discipleship makes sense only in the context of a community of faith that supports the believer in her effort to be faithful. Readers from both Anabaptist and non-Anabaptist traditions should find this book helpful for dialogue in the search for consistent ways to follow Scripture in economic life.

1

The Economic Context

Economics exists because we live in a world of scarcity. This is true no matter where we live, what century we live in, or how plentiful our resources are. To illustrate how pervasive scarcity is, imagine a world where there is an abundance of everything and all resources are free. What will you do? No doubt you will act like the shopper who can have anything at zero price so long as he selects and brings it to the checkout counter in fifteen minutes. The shopper immediately experiences a strong sense of scarcity even though all the products are free. Why? Because suddenly *time* is scarce and must be allocated carefully. If he ends up with the perfect market basket, it is because—perhaps unconsciously—he used sound economic reasoning in allocating his time. Only in a timeless heaven is economics obsolete.

If we give the shopper two constraints, the problem more closely approximates the real world. Suppose that he has fifteen minutes, one hundred dollars, and cannot ignore prices. Now the venture becomes more difficult; more decisions are necessary. Time is scarce and resources are scarce—a fact communicated by their having prices. Scarcity in this example illustrates the dilemma that we all find ourselves in every day. We have limited time and resources, while our imaginations can dream up endless wants to fulfill. This condition is as true for twentieth-century Americans as it was for the ancient world of the Hebrews and the first-century world of Jesus. The economic problem is universal.

To say we live in a world of scarcity is not to say that the world is incapable of providing enough to keep humanity alive and well.

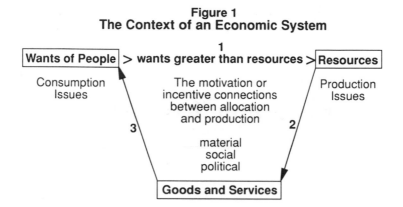

Figure 1
The Context of an Economic System

Rather, it means that people cannot have all they desire at a price they can afford. In a world where people's wants are minimal and their productivity high, scarcity could be eliminated. However, that world has not yet been found. I suggest later in this book that Christian people should develop the concept of limited wants, but the controversy that this suggestion usually creates among believers is proof enough that a secular concept of limited wants is far from a reality.

Economic decisions, then, are made within the framework of scarcity. Any system must allocate limited resources among an endless list of desires in ways that are consistent with the values of the society, foster adequate production, and accommodate needed change. All systems, whether for small groups or large nations, must deal with these issues if they hope to survive.

It is helpful at this point to depict the requirements of an economic system (see fig. 1). The upper two boxes illustrate that people live in a world of scarcity. They have endless wants and limited resources and time, so they must find a way to cope with the problem. Three major ways present themselves. First, a partial solution would be to scale down the wants to make the gap between wants and resources feel smaller. If society moved toward a simple-life-style norm that made minimal resource use socially desirable, the gap between wants and available resources would become smaller. Since per capita economic growth was not an expected outcome of economic behavior throughout most of history, it is easy to understand why Jesus, in the first century, was oriented more toward conservation and redistribution than toward expanded production. Second, the production process, which takes basic resources and generates usable goods and services, can be developed and perfected in order to stretch the basic resources as far as they can go. Third, the method of allocating available goods and services among consumers can be improved so that products go to their best uses.

It is important to understand the three components of this economic context triangle. Each side has its own set of issues.

Side 1 deals with all the concerns associated with scaling down *living standards* and coping with a steady-state economic environment. In most societies this conservation approach is not popular because it is thought to cause unemployment or, at least, slow economic growth. In the secular world of western market capitalism, where desires are an individual matter and personal autonomy is a primary goal, most people prefer more to less. Countering this natural tendency is considered an unacceptable act of coercion. Consequently, the secular mindset does not view the alternative of a simpler life as a viable option. This option will be considered later when we look at Christian alternatives.

Side 2 of the triangle deals with issues of *production* economics. Discovering more resources and processing them more effectively are the tasks of those who tackle the scarcity problem from this angle. The technological change and constantly expanding productivity of the modern world help make this option seem plausible.

Side 3 is concerned with finding the best way to get goods and services to their best uses in *consumption*. It has to do with how goods and services are distributed among the millions of people who want them. Why should this home go to this family and not to that? Why should that pair of slacks go to that consumer and not to another? How best can we determine who ought to enjoy a given service of which there isn't enough for everyone?

Both the production and the consumption sides of the triangle must deal with problems of *allocation*, since production requires inputs to be put to their best uses. In fact, economics as a discipline is really the study of ways to tie together the entire triangle into a system that allocates scarce resources and products to make them serve people. In much of the western world, that system is

democratic capitalism, a system often unfairly maligned, sometimes oversold, and usually only vaguely understood. For Christians, for whom biblical teaching is an important ingredient
conditioning the triangle, special challenges exist in making the
allocation processes depicted by the triangle Christian in
character. This challenge is the topic of chapters 4–7.

In the Middle Ages the triangle was coordinated by social, political, and religious obligations, responsibilities, and rights that
created a static social structure. This system appears like a stag-
nant dark age to those accustomed to rapid change and progress,
but it did provide social stability for many centuries.

In the earlier period of Roman rule, the triangle was organized
by the law of a central authority, from which subjects deviated at
their own risk. In Jesus' day, economic behavior was controlled by
power beyond the control of the Jewish people, who were forced to
sacrifice to Rome most of any significant surplus they could generate. Thus the believer's economic behavior occurred in a framework of very limited options. The persecuted believer was even
more confined in the alternatives available to solve economic
problems. The teachings of Jesus and the New Testament writers
are best understood against this backdrop.

In the ancient Hebrew world of the Old Testament the economic
triangle was dealt with in the context of a community of faith. A
theocracy with revealed law, a prescribed social organization, and
a covenant relationship with Yahweh answered the economic
questions in some detail.

Thus history proceeds from one perspective to another, always
facing the same issues of scarcity and allocation. The answers
come out in different ways, but the Christian always desires to
bridge the gap between the ancient and the modern in ways that
fulfill the wishes of the Creator, the only constant in the long flow
of history.

The next chapter explores sides 2 and 3 of this triangle to give a
clearer perspective on the issues involved in allocation for production and consumption. Chapters 3–7 suggest an approach to the
economic triangle that reflects kingdom-of-God values. Chapters
8–11 explain how market capitalism deals with the economic
triangle and contrast the Christian model with the secular system. Chapter 12 attempts to deal with these contrasts in a way

that can help believers bridge the gap between the world's values and their Christian values.

Discussion Questions

1. Is it true that people of all income levels and social structures feel a constant sense of shortage, whether of things or of time?
2. Is it a Christian virtue to be satisfied and stop striving for more?

Allocation of Resources

Let's continue the discussion of the economic triangle by exploring more fully the process of allocation for consumption. Picture yourself back in the early 1970s during the oil embargo. You are a gas station attendant with a long line of customers. You have only one hundred gallons left in your supply tank, and ten cars are lined up, each needing fifteen gallons. You have an economic problem on your hands: you need a system to allocate the limited supply of fuel. What alternatives are available?

Deciding Who Gets What

First, you might use a first-come, first-served method. You might simply keep pumping until the seventh car exhausts the supply of gas. The remaining three cars get nothing. Whether the tenth car is an ambulance, or a police car, or driven by someone enroute to the hospital for emergency care, it will not be serviced. This first-come, first-served method places the highest value on being early.

A second system might be to allocate based on need. In this case you would ask all drivers how they intended to use the gas and then decide, either by yourself or through a democratic process of voting or polling, how the gas should be divided. This system assumes that people have a generally accepted view of what need is and are prepared to live with the consequences of the allocation. Under this system everyone has an incentive to appear most needy. If need is related to low income, there is incentive to be—or at least to appear—poor.

A third method of allocation is simply to give everyone in the line an equal share of gasoline, no matter where they are in line or what their need is. This system puts a high value on equal treatment of everyone so there is no reason to be early in line or to project a position of need. But it also faces difficulty in maintaining equality when, after serving one customer or more, someone new joins the line.

A fourth way of solving the problem is cronyism. In this system, the supplier identifies his regular customers or friends and gives them fuel. This gives people incentive to seek friendships with people of power and wealth. Political patronage and conformity to the wishes of those with resources characterize a system based on cronyism.

Another allocative process is open conflict. If the people waiting for gasoline became irate and feared losing their source of transportation, fights could erupt and the victor could have the fuel. This chaotic approach usually erupts when a society's institutional structures are so weak or unfair that people take matters into their own hands.

One other method of resource allocation is the auction, in which those who bid highest get the most gasoline. In this system, it is important to have enough money to bid to the level required to get the desired quantities of gasoline. Except for the cases of inherited wealth or unmerited windfall income, the money one has to bid with presumably comes from wages in the labor auction. Thus one's work effort is directly related to the amount of gas one can buy. This *link between allocation and production* is unique among all the methods discussed.

During the oil embargo, virtually every method described above was used somewhere in the country. In an overall economy, one method or another dominates economic exchange. In the United States the auction method prevails. The fact that bidders and sellers exchange freely makes this method appealing to a democratic tradition. In other parts of the world, where populations lack the sophistication and social support structures of low-cost communication, information, transportation, and political stability, the auction allocation mechanism works far less effectively. In societies with a tradition of centralized governmental power or a dominant leader, a method that relies on the leader's choices—what we described above as cronyism—is usually popular.

No matter which system a society uses, it must deal with the forces of supply and demand. If an auction isn't used, the people who wait in line pay in money plus time rather than just money. The king who allocates to his cronies pays in reduced political support from the masses, who pay in reduced political and personal choice. In short, a price is paid whenever scarce resources are allocated, though the effects differ depending on the method used.

Motivations to Produce

Because the consumption process is only one side of the economic triangle, we need to expand our discussion to include issues related to production as well. Unfortunately many Christians consider economic systems only as consumption processes and find the methods of allocation based on need and equality more appealing than the auction method. The appeal of these methods derives from biblical teaching that abhors extremes of wealth and poverty and advocates an ethic of service to the poor as central to the gospel. A relevant question might be, "Should Christian people operate with one allocative method in the community of faith and another in dealing with the world at large?" Before we take up that question in chapter 6, we need to gain further insight into what makes an economic system work.

The output of goods and services that a society can produce in any given time depends on the resources and technology available and on the world view of the people. Before discussing these technical, socioreligious, and natural factors involved in production, we need to consider incentives for people to produce. People must have a reason to replace leisure with work if they are to produce goods and services. Incentives can come in at least three forms.

First is the material factor. If someone is rewarded for work with resources or money to buy resources, she will work as long as she considers the rewards worth more than the leisure she gives up. Since the auction, or market, system ties a person's standard of living to her work effort, that system is ideal for societies that put top priority on high living standards. However, it is wrong to assume that other allocative systems have no material incentives to work. If a society produces only enough for subsistence, the alternative to work is starvation—a strong incentive to work even if the worker receives only a small share of the output.

A second motivation for work is the social and psychological benefit one derives from it. If work provides a creative outlet for one's abilities, and if one finds satisfaction in the group aspects of work, he can be highly productive regardless of whether payment is proportionate to output. Volunteers and people who accept less than they could earn elsewhere work because of this type of motivation.

A third motivation might come from political pressure to produce. A system that requires specified amounts of output under threat of penalty or that espouses production goals to which people willingly strive because they embrace its political goals uses this motivation.

All three of these motivations may be present simultaneously in any system, but usually one motivation dominates. The capitalistic western world operates primarily on the belief that material rewards can keep productivity high. The social motivation is considered desirable but is viewed as weaker and is often traded away if material gains compete with social goals. In other words, people often reject meaningful and fulfilling but low-paying work to accept jobs that are less desirable except for the higher pay.

In short, capitalists believe that people behave as if they are motivated mainly by the prospect of material rewards and that any system that does not give full recognition to that fact will be doomed to low production, a low standard of living, and, therefore, an inferior existence.[1] Given this perspective, the only allocation

---

1. Adam Smith (in the eighteenth century) argued that nonmaterial considerations can be as powerful as material ones, or even more powerful. Smith, in *The Theory of Moral Sentiments* (Indianapolis: Liberty Classics, 1976), presented justice, benevolence, and prudence as the three primary motivations of all human action, and analyzed the desire for honor, respect, advancement in society, wealth, and other motivations as subsets of those. In the late nineteenth century and throughout the twentieth, thinkers identified as members of the Austrian School of Economics have emphasized the idea that incentive includes anything a person desires, whether material or nonmaterial, whether selfish or self-sacrificial. One representative of that school, Ludwig von Mises, develops these ideas in *Human Action: A Treatise on*

and production mechanism that makes sense is the market price or auction system. To the capitalist, only this system can deliver the goods and preserve freedom.

The most prominent alternative to capitalism is Marxist socialism. Its many varieties throughout the world hold a common view regarding the motivation to produce. Marxism claims to see historical progression in human society. Initially people are selfish, driven by material desires. When they are placed in a capitalist setting and given license to acquire as much as possible, large inequalities develop. These must strain the legitimacy of any system until it collapses in chaotic conflict. Marxists believe that people will learn from that experience and move to a higher level of motivation: the desire to contribute to the welfare of society and the common good. This new motivation makes production for material gain obsolete. Allocation is done according to need. This must lead to an egalitarian society in which authoritarian structures eventually fade away.

As with other systems based on an optimistic view of human nature, history has not verified Marxist theory. Instead, the social motivation to solve allocation and production problems collec-

---

Economics, 3d rev. ed. (Chicago: Regnery, 1966). Evangelical philosopher Ronald Nash discusses this point extensively in *Poverty and Wealth: The Christian Debate Over Capitalism* (Westchester, Ill.: Crossway, 1986), chap. 4, "The Theory of Subjective Economic Value." Such thinkers tend to see material rewards as only intermediate and desirable only to the extent that they are means to the fulfillment of persons' nonmaterial goals (happiness, charity toward others, learning).

All of this may be true, but these arguments serve to make capitalist behavior more justifiable rather than to refute the idea that capitalism allocates goods and services efficiently because material rewards are pursued as the key means to the good life. Common perceptions that profits are needed to drive the system and that lower taxes will increase the work effort further support the view presented in this book. The fact that increased profits or take-home pay might be donated to the church does not alter the fact that the desire for material rewards drives the system. Whether profits are a primary goal or simply a means to charitable activity is irrelevant to the functioning of the system, even though they are important considerations in assessing its moral character. It is a bit ironic that some who argue the loudest against the notion that capitalism is driven by the desire for material gain often use the high level of material well-being of the capitalist societies as proof of the superiority of market capitalism. A system should be evaluated on how well it delivers on the goals it seeks to achieve. Few if any studies compare systems by looking at the values put forth by Smith, von Mises, and Nash.

tively gives way to a coercive political system that forces a centrally planned production and distribution schedule on its people. Thus, in the effort to develop an ideal system, Marxist societies often lose both basic freedom and efficiency.

The Christian's work is motivated by both of these incentives. Scripture encourages work for material sufficiency; self-actualization and social interaction also are worthy reasons to work. But the Christian has at least two additional motives for work. The first is the desire to serve those who need help by giving either income or labor. The second is the desire to use the workplace for witness and mission. Infiltrating the work environment for the cause of the gospel may not reform the world, but it can serve as salt and light to others and attract some to faith.

Indeed, these last two motivations should play a more important role in the believer's productive activity than the material rewards that dominate the work decisions of the majority of the population. The believer should not need a system driven by material benefits for high productivity.

Making Production Decisions

Once the motivation to produce is understood, it is necessary to explore what economists call the production function. Although this typically refers to the relationship between physical inputs and outputs, it is useful to broaden the scope of analysis to include both tangible and intangible inputs to and outputs of the process.

Tangible Factors in the Economy

Tangible inputs are easily listed: land, labor, capital, and entrepreneurship all are woven into a process that generates output. Any production effort must determine how these inputs are combined for maximum efficiency. This is an enormously complex problem because inputs often can substitute for each other. A bushel of wheat could be produced on one hundred square feet of land with a ton of fertilizer, a mechanical robot, and one hour of human labor, or it could be produced with one acre of land and one hundred hours of human labor. Which is better? The same question could be asked of alternative ways of teaching students, curing patients, making automobiles, or cutting hair.

The answer is the economist's standard answer to most question: *It all depends.* It all depends on how plentiful or scarce the various resources are. If robots and fertilizer are hard to find but land is plentiful, the second way of growing wheat makes more sense than the first. Unfortunately, there are far more than two ways of growing wheat. In fact, millions of different combinations of the inputs could work. Deciding which is best is more difficult than it first appears.

Maybe the place to begin understanding production is with another question: Who should evaluate all the data to see which input allocations are best? This brings us to another set of alternatives similar to those we considered in the discussion of methods of allocation for consumption. First, we might appoint some person or group to be in charge of production, to research all the questions and answer them as best it can. By planning how much of all goods and services should be produced and the methods required to produce them, the group could attempt to steer society toward its goal. In addition, the planners would need to define, on the allocation side, what need and equality really mean. Good planners would listen closely to the wishes of the people so that the production and distribution questions were answered in socially desirable ways. If they failed, they might be fired—unless they had political power of dictatorial proportions, in which case only political revolution could remove them.

A second method of answering the production questions is the same auction environment discussed in the consumption section. Everyone with something to contribute to production offers it for sale if he chooses to. People offer their labor. Mine owners offer their coal. Land owners offer land for sale or rent. People with extra funds offer them as loans to others who need extra money at the auction. As the auction proceeds, people listen to the auctioneer and alter their decisions in response to changing prices. For example, the journalist homemaker might hunt a baby sitter so that she would be free to enter the labor auction if the wage rate for journalists went high enough to attract her. People might adjust their spending and save more if the interest rate rose in the loanable funds market. Farmers might use less land and more fertilizer if land prices soared. These auctions are continuous and, in the process, people receive or lose income as they offer skills and resources for sale. Also, producers respond to the price signals, choosing the collection of inputs available for production. In other words, *it all depends* on the prices of the inputs, which depend on the supply and demand of each resource in its respective auction.

If the production market is brought together with the allocation market, exchange activity goes on continuously with people receiving and spending money and reacting to market signals. All the while, the questions of what is produced, how it is produced, and who gets the production are being answered by the millions of decisions buyers and sellers—consumers and producers—are making. This is the essence of a market economy. It sounds like a cumbersome process, but remember: the questions it is answering are extremely complex.

Intangible Factors in the Economy

The preceding discussion illustrates the tangible, technical side of production. Overlaying these technical considerations of production are the intangible issues of values, religion, ethics, and justice. Many studies show that these intangible factors heavily condition the technical outcomes.

For example, before the Reformation, the church taught against the desire to acquire riches. Later, during the Reformation, many secular occupations that had been viewed as spiritually inferior to church work became acceptable as callings from God. The more communal focus of feudal life styles gave way to the elevation of individual pursuit. The desire to acquire and seek social advancement was no longer considered a sin, as the medieval world had seen it. Clearly, entrepreneurial economic activity gradually was becoming acceptable to God, at least from the point of view of the sixteenth-century Christian.

One writer illustrates this well:

> The world of Today elbowed aside the world of Tomorrow, and as life on earth became more important, so did the notion of material standards and ordinary comforts. Behind the change in religious tolerance was the rise of Protestantism, which hastened a new attitude toward work and wealth. . . . Acquisitiveness became a recognized virtue—not immediately for one's private enjoyment,

but for the greater glory of God. From here it was only a step to the identification of riches with spiritual excellence, and of rich men with saintly ones.[2]

Social customs as well as religious values sometimes constrain production behavior. Some societies' values prevent women from seeking employment. In other cultures, racial discrimination or concern for income disparities limit certain production or consumption options.

In every society, the list of intangibles ultimately combines with the technical factors to form the social fabric out of which an economic system is formed. It is a mistake to evaluate any economic system on the technical variables alone. Free-market outcomes may appear ideal to a capitalist in the United States, but they may appear wrong to a member of the labor party in the Netherlands who is willing to trade some of his standard of living in order to adopt some economic planning that he believes will give more people jobs.

Costs and Benefits of Planning and Markets

No system is either all market oriented or all centrally planned. Planned production and allocation do occur in a capitalist society. Thus the real problem is determining where planning stops and markets begin.

Examples may be helpful here. In the home, family members don't bid for the food, clothing, and shelter available, and the tasks of production are usually planned in some sense. In general, parents are the central planners. They make decisions for the children, allocating the resources according to some value system that, it is to be hoped, everyone perceives to be fair. Business enterprises, too, are usually centrally planned by the owners and managers so that complicated auction arrangements need not be set up for routine activities. In general, central planning is preferred when the costs of organizing effective auctions are greater than the benefits the markets bring to the participants.

---

2. Robert L. Heilbroner, *The Worldly Philosophers: The Lives, Times, and Ideas of the Great Economic Thinkers,* 5th ed. (New York: Simon and Schuster, 1980), pp. 32–33.

The case of college class registration can be illustrative here. The University of Chicago Business School distributes coupons, or pretend money, to its students each year. They can use the coupons to bid on classes they want to take. These coupons become bidding rights, a type of property right. The highest bidders get the class slots that are most in demand. Students must choose how to spend their coupons in ways that will bring them the most desired course schedules.

At Wheaton College we allocate class slots differently. No auction exists. Students simply stand in line and a first-come, first-served policy of allocation prevails. We impose a value system that says seniors get first place in the line and freshmen must go last. In the end students seem to get the courses they want over a four-year period, but there is less of an auction environment and more of an administratively planned atmosphere. Both systems finally produce graduates, but the selection process of course inputs differs.

Some time ago in a conversation with University of Chicago students and faculty who were discussing the bidding process, students were lamenting the fact that no futures market exists in coupons and that their freedom was therefore limited. After observing the energy spent on constructing the market environment of class registration, I commented that it might be much simpler to have a first-come, first-served method like most other schools use. One person responded that the value of freedom is high and needs to be protected at all cost.

The moral of this story is not that one side was for free markets and the other for central planning. Rather, it was that I felt freedom by being released from the confusion of constructing and participating in registration markets, while they felt more freedom by being released from an imposed first-come, first-served system. No wonder families, firms, and countries prefer planning for some activities instead of the perpetual negotiating of a market environment. Markets are not costless. Some people prefer to avoid the cost of markets by sacrificing freedom for central organization.

But central planning is not costless either. As already mentioned, people who accept planning sacrifice some freedom. They may also sacrifice efficiency. This is more obvious as the operation under consideration becomes larger and larger.

The manager of a small manufacturing company may efficiently plan the flow of labor, raw materials, and capital in his production process, but for someone to organize the flow of these resources throughout an entire society would be an enormous task requiring so much information as to be impossible at any cost. At some point it becomes apparent that markets can generate, collect, and process the required information through their pricing mechanism better than any planner. At that point markets become the appropriate mechanism to allocate the resources.

In general, the better educated people are, the more developed the vehicles for information flow, the more mobile the resources within a society, and the more numerous the buyers and sellers, the lower will be the cost of the market process. This is especially so if these characteristics also lead toward independent thinking that resists the coercive aspects of planning.

Once again, the question for the Christian might be whether resource owners—including laborers—should be paid according to the market price signals of society or by some other method. The model developed in chapter 6 argues for market-resource pricing but makes a strong distinction between income and use of that income in consumption.

Conclusions: Moving Beyond the Socialist-Capitalist Debate

History shows that markets organize economic resources far better than planners.[3] The incentives to produce that the auction method of allocation provides have been so powerful that western economists generally have disdained central planning at the national level. Consequently, many capitalists have endorsed the recent effort to remove more government control from economic life.

Although the efficiency question is important, the more intense and emotional issue related to planning is the concern for freedom. At what point does one cross the line into oppression? Surely, children who resist the structure of parental authority are

3. Peter L. Berger, *The Capitalist Revolution: Fifty Propositions About Prosperity, Equality, and Liberty* (New York: Basic Books, 1986), p. 211.

carrying freedom to the extreme. The students at the University of Chicago might build a compelling freedom case for auction registration, but few other students in the country have thought it important enough to seek changes in registration procedures. Only at more complex levels of resource organization is there more generalized consensus that planning is inevitably a serious threat to freedom.

Probably very few Christian economists would argue for a centrally planned economic system for any country, even fewer would espouse it for developed countries where highly advanced education, communication, and transportation provide fairly low-cost information channels for markets to use. Certainly, the democratic, free-enterprise, individualistic tradition in the United States is hostile to central planning in economic affairs where markets can operate effectively.

If it is true that few Christian economists support centrally planned economies, the capitalist-socialist debate that has attracted intense concern for some observers should be refocused. This task will be taken up again in later chapters when we explore capitalism in more detail. I hope it will become clear that the policy debates among economists often focus on the strategies for dealing with the shortcomings of the market process. These strategies usually are designed to improve rather than to destroy a market system. This means that the relevant area of debate is not socialism vs. capitalism, but the appropriate type of government involvement that the market environment needs to be most effective and viable.

The discussion so far has hinted that Christians follow a higher calling than do non-Christians, although very few specifics have been developed. I have implied that Christians are to live in ways that point toward the coming kingdom of God and are to call the world around them toward a new life. The concepts of allocation and production in an environment of scarcity cannot be forgotten, but believers are called to handle these concerns in uniquely Christian ways. What is the quality of this new life?

Discussion Questions

1. Of all the methods of allocation, are there some that feel more Christian or less Christian than others? Why?

2. Is it true, as this chapter argues, that allocation systems cannot be evaluated purely on how Christian they appear to be, but also on how well they structure incentives that will contribute to additional production?

3. Is it necessary for Christian people to have the material–reward incentive in order to be productive, or is working a natural response to God's gift of resources and grace?

4. Illustrate, with examples from various cultures, the three motivations to work. Are there others that should be added?

5. What do R. H. Tawney in *Religion and the Rise of Capitalism* and Max Weber in *The Protestant Ethic and the Spirit of Capitalism* add to the discussion on the role of religion in economic activity? (Explore these books for the answer.)

6. If optimal production input combinations depend on the relative scarcity of the factors of production more than on the conclusions of intelligent engineers, what strategy for third world economic development would you recommend?

7. Why might someone argue that auction class registration will lead to better classes than a first-come, first-served method? (This is a hard question with answers that relate to better faculty and student class preparation.)

8. Can you explain why markets tend to be less costly in developed countries than in less developed countries?

3

Biblical Background
to Economic Thinking

Economic concerns are always prominent in the history of a people. Certainly this was true in Hebrew life as depicted in the Old Testament and in the Christian era of the New Testament. To be understood properly, Old Testament law must be studied in its theological and sociological setting. The Hebrew people of the ancient mideast were not just another group of nomads vying for the limited space of the fertile crescent. On the contrary, God had called them to a special task in history and had provided guidance to them in their mission. The guidance God provided has become source material for twentieth-century Christians, but it is not easy for us to understand and apply it.

Judaic law specified behavior in the context of a covenant relationship in which the people were required to maintain a specific social structure. It is in this structure that the law made sense and could be applied meaningfully. Superimposing the behavioral part of the law on an alien social structure can lead to perverse outcomes.

For example, the social-welfare function of gleaning in the Hebrew system is more easily abused in an individual entrepreneurial environment than in a caring, community-oriented social structure. Millard Lind, in a paper on the economics of the Hebrews, refers to this process of applying Hebrew law to alien social environments as "cream skimming" theology from the text.[1] "Cream skimming" can occur when economists attempt to remove the enlightenment philosophical underpinnings from contemporary democratic capitalism and replace them with the philosophy of Old Testament law.

For example, the suggestion that education for all is a modern application of the jubilee principle (Lev. 25) has a certain appeal. However, if schools simply educate students in ways that do not reduce socioeconomic disparities, then the redistributive effects of education may be far less than hoped for. A substantial literature questions the redistributive effects of elementary and secondary education in the United States. It may be impossible to graft the jubilee concept into American economic life as long as individual freedom and competition are fundamental to our social and economic organization. Social structure and theology come as a package and cannot easily be separated.[2]

---

1. Millard Lind, "The Economics of the Hebrews," an unpublished paper presented at the Regional Consultation on the Meaning and Importance of Money in Following Jesus, September 1980, p. 1.

2. There is some question whether the jubilee principle was specifically designed as a redistribution instrument or a limitation on irresponsible borrowing. If the land that was transferred to someone else for a time was merely collateral for a loan, and if the size of the loan was limited to the expected return from that land between the time of the transfer and the jubilee year, then the return of the land is merely a return of the collateral after a loan is retired. E. Calvin Beisner presents this view in *Prosperity and Poverty: The Compassionate Use of Resources in a World of Scarcity* (Westchester, Ill.: Crossway, 1988), chapter 5. Beisner states that "the provisions of the jubilee year were designed not to promote economic equality but to prevent one family member's destroying an entire family's means of productivity, not only in his own generation but also in generations to come, by selling, permanently, the family's means of production." This interesting interpretation, rather than arguing against a redistributive focus of the jubilee, actually provides a more forceful case for God's interest in income redistribution. God programed into the structure a mechanism that acted as a deterrent to destitution even across generations. By restricting the borrowing of one party the jubilee also restricted the lending ability of another party that had a differing view of present and future income. This prevents what otherwise may become larger income disparities over time. Effective income redistribution mechanisms need not be pure income transfers, although many think of them in those terms. A preferred way of dealing with inequities is to build in structural safeguards against the poverty-causing process. Indeed, there is no way to divorce the jubilee concept completely from redistribution considerations, but it is important to see it as part of the entire Hebrew social system that is discussed later in this chapter.

A preferred approach is to come at the issue from the other direction, exploring first the social structure that is most suited to the entire biblical record and then how we might change the social structure to conform more closely to the teachings of Scripture. To proceed in this venture, we must recognize first that the law came to a theocratic society that God had chosen to work out his unique purposes. The counterpart in our contemporary world is the church, not any secular state or social group. Therefore, the biblical content speaks first to the church, and a Christian economics must reflect the kind of economic relationships and behavior that is normative for believers as a body.

Biblical Norms and Counterculture

The claim that social structures condition behavior does not mean that a community of faith must have a social structure like that of the people of God in Bible times if it is to be faithful to Scripture. Rather, it means that social organization among believers must have characteristics that are compatible with the core teaching in Scripture on economic relationships, even if the surrounding society accepts another kind of social pattern. This two-kingdom view of God's work in the world will be developed later, but it is important to emphasize here that this approach views God as working on two fronts in creation and the church as having a special place in his plans.

Certainly all of creation is God's domain and ultimately serves his purposes. Nevertheless, he has selected those who come to faith as special witnesses to the radical calling that brings him special glory. The biblical record reveals that calling and shows how faithfulness to it is the best evangelistic message to the secular world. We shortchange the message of the gospel and the witness of the church when we start from any secular social and economic system and attempt to leaven it with a piecemeal application of biblical principles while ignoring the far-reaching social implications of the Scripture. Ultimately, the believer is an alien and stranger in the secular world; his involvement with it is like that of a traveler in a foreign land. Obviously he must interact with the secular system, but his focus is on the new life that cannot be understood by the unbeliever unless he comes to faith.

The social and economic system of the Hebrews differed dramatically from anything around them. The Egyptian monarchy and the city-states of Palestine were highly centralized in structure. Excessive service and wealth were given to royalty. Slavery and class distinctions were the norm, and power and violent force were the tools of social order. A weak king and ineffective military meant almost certain social chaos or takeover by an outside power. Lesser nations sought, through alliances or tribute payments, to maintain autonomy as long as possible, but loyalty to agreements meant little when alternative opportunity appeared. Income distribution was, by design, very unequal. Challenging this way of doing things made little sense since no alternatives seemed practical.

Into this world God called a people and presented them with values that seemed hopelessly radical. First, there was to be no king. The entire pyramid of power was inverted so that the household, rather than the royalty, became the focus of attention. The family, clan, tribe, and nation were designed to support the household in all affairs of life. Figure 2 illustrates the way in which the social structure was put together. Alternative models were employed by the Hebrews throughout their history. The exodus and wilderness experiences were clearly more nomadic than the picture of Hebrew life presented here. Likewise, God did not reject the reign of the kings. However, the wanderings and the royalty experiences were aberrations from God's design for his people. The prophetic critique of kingship and the fact that much of the wilderness experience was punishment are evidence for this view.

Perhaps the Book of Ruth is the most beautiful example of how this social system was supposed to work. Naomi and her family left Judah during a famine and took up residence in Moab, a neighboring country. There Naomi's husband and two sons died, leaving her with two Moabite daughters-in-law, one of whom, Ruth, returned to Judah with her. Then the family or clan of Naomi's deceased husband began the process of restoring Naomi into the system by applying biblical norms.

The process began with Ruth's gleaning and ended with Boaz's purchase of Naomi's land and marriage to Ruth. At the birth of Ruth's first son the process of being restored to the fold of Israel was complete. The social system had worked, as witnessed by Naomi's friends, who said, "Praise be to the LORD, who this day

Figure 2
Hebrew Social Structure

Nation

Tribe—identity of the tribe depended on the success of the family household

Family—served the welfare and insurance function 100–1000 people

Household 8–100 people

The social structure had the larger units serving the smaller units rather than the usual reverse pattern.

has not left you without a kinsman-redeemer" (Ruth 4:14). It is no accident that the term used for kinsman-redeemer in this Hebrew text is parallel to the Greek word for ransom, which is used to describe the redemptive work of Christ in Mark 10:35. God wants social structures to protect against destitution and alienation. Apparently, a decentralized web of mutual responsibility and accountability among all groupings of society was God's design for his people, rather than the topdown, royalty-to-serf structure of Israel's contemporaries or the individualized responsibility and accountability of our modern western world.

It seems that God's intentions for his people were radically countercultural in many respects, and his covenant with the Hebrews required that they be faithful to his expectations if they were to receive his blessing and protection. The Hebrews' repeated unfaithfulness is not surprising in view of the radical nature of God's wishes, and so the constant refrain of Scripture tells of God's calling his people back to himself and his ways. From Genesis to Revelation we read of God's people following other gods and of God's calling them back through prophets, preachers, and circumstances. Throughout history, God continues to call his people back to practices that seem utopian to anyone heavily involved in the world. That the Hebrews never were able to free themselves from the desire to be like others, the Old Testament documents. That this desire is a timeless temptation is a thesis of this book, as is the notion that the temptation is nearly impossible to resist without a supporting community of faith.

While the Old Testament prophets strongly criticized patterns of behavior that broke down the web of protection against poverty, they do not appear to have indicted generalized prosperity. The Old Testament is full of examples of God blessing his people materially. In these cases, however, there is an underlying confidence that, if the law is kept, the social structure will filter out the dangers of wealth accumulation. Apparently Boaz was wealthy, but he used his wealth to carry out the intent of the law. The same is true of many Old Testament persons, although—as in the case of Solomon—the temptations of wealth and power were too great for some.

Later Jewish Teaching

Jewish teaching since Old Testament times has sought, through legal codes, communal legislation, and religious literature, to condition economic behavior. No economic system is endorsed or condemned in Judaic teaching. However, there is a clear expectation that all systems should conform to religious constraints. Meir Tamari, in *With All Your Possessions*, describes limitations that Judaism places on economic activity.

1. There is a limitation on the time allowed for economic activity, because of the obligation to study Torah.
2. The production or sale of goods or services that are harmful to their consumers, either physically or morally, is forbidden.
3. One is responsible for damages caused by one's body or property.
4. Theft or economic dishonesty in any form or guise is forbidden.
5. One is required to limit one's appetite for material goods. One's disposable income is also automatically reduced by the demands of *tzedakah* (social welfare) and interest-free loans, and by taxation to finance welfare, education, and the physical well-being of the community.[3]

---

3. Meir Tamari, *With All Your Possessions: Jewish Ethics and Economic Activity* (New York: Free Press, 1987), p. 59.

The specific directives relating to each of these limitations make it clear that religious concerns were of first importance in Jewish teaching over the centuries. One example of how this teaching affected behavior can be seen in regard to the first limitation. Since any time spent in economic life detracted from study of the Torah, there is a bias against occupations that do not have considerable flex-time built in. Consequently, a recurring theme in Jewish teaching encourages commerce rather than farming as an occupation because commerce allows more time for religious study.[4]

The Messianic Mission of Jesus

By the time the New Testament writers came on the scene a great deal had changed. The concept of Israel as an eminent, politically autonomous power or mini-power had faded for all but the Zealots. The Romans, though outwardly detested by most of their subjects, had brought considerable political stability to the Mediterranean world and allowed limited governing rights to the local groups under their control. Within Israel the hope for the promised Messiah was still nurtured, and that hope was cast in terms of a political resurgence, but few saw any simple divine escape from Rome.

Into this climate came John the Baptist and then Jesus with a strange and confusing message. Jesus' message was so unusual that the devil tried to sidetrack him into a more conventional messianic strategy. After Jesus was baptized he went into the wilderness. There he fought off the temptation to carry out the messianic responsibilities in economic, political, and established religious ways. When he began to pursue the suffering-servant way of the cross, the alienation process began that led to Calvary and death. Apart from the resurrection, Jesus is little more than a wise teacher with some unique powers. But the resurrection did occur, and thus the story of God's work in the world goes on.[5]

---

4. Ibid., p. 28.

5. For a sociological study of the New Testament world read Derek Tidball, *The Social Context of the New Testament: A Sociological Analysis* (Grand Rapids: Zondervan, 1984).

Jesus, to the disappointment of many, did not speak of the kingdom of God as a theocracy of the Jews. In fact, he discussed politics very little in a direct sense. For him, the kingdom of God was a way of life for believers in community.

What this means for the economic relationships of believers in the modern world is the next topic of the book. We will look at it in three parts: the first deals with the movement of the work of God from the theocracy of Israel to the believer's church; the second interprets New Testament passages on wealth and income in light of the modern capital-oriented market economy; and the third sketches what economic relationships among believers ought to be like.

The law of Moses looked forward to something more inclusive and complete, something Jesus called the kingdom of God. In Christ God's plan for people came to fruition. His effort to communicate the significance of God's kingdom became the major part of his ministry. The establishment of the church was an important step in fleshing out that kingdom in the world.

Discussion Questions

1. Do you agree with Lind's assessment that Christians have tried to "cream skim" theology out of Scripture and ignored the implications of the text on social structures? Support your answer with examples.
2. Is it appropriate to infuse a social structure designed for a theocracy on a secular social environment? If so, give examples where such a process has been successful. If not, does one apply the social principles to the church or not at all?
3. Is it possible that an application of the social principles of the Hebrews, if applied by the community of believers today, would be a form of witness and evangelism?
4. Could you write a research paper on how the church related biblical teaching to social structures throughout the middle ages? Ideally this history would be an important, and lengthy, addition to this chapter.

4

The Two-Kingdom Approach to the Bible

One of the most exciting and frightening realizations that comes from a casual reading of the New Testament is that the kingdom of God already was being established, in part, on earth in the first century. Matthew 12:28 associates Christ's exorcism of demons with the coming of the kingdom, suggesting that it had already broken through and was seeking citizens willing to identify with it. That God had broken directly into history and was building the kingdom is exciting, but a more penetrating look at the kind of kingdom he was building is frightening. The kingdom demands a high level of commitment from the believer. Throughout the New Testament, the terms *kingdom of God* and *kingdom of heaven* are used synonymously, and together the passages form a composite that is worthy of careful attention from all Christians.

Theologians from early Christianity to the present have struggled with the meaning of the term *kingdom of God*. A typical definition calls the kingdom

> the sovereign rule of God manifested in Christ to defeat His enemies creating a people over whom He reigns, and issuing in a realm or realms in which the power of His reign is experienced. All they are members of the kingdom of God who voluntarily submit to the rule of God in their lives. Entrance into the kingdom is by the new birth (John 3:3–5); two stages are in the kingdom of God: present and future in an eschatological sense.[1]

1. Edward Viening, ed., *The Zondervan Topical Bible* (Grand Rapids: Zondervan, 1969), p. 608.

Questions arise because there seems to be a progressive sense in which the reign of Christ is fulfilled. The present and future characteristics of the kingdom have been interpreted differently over the centuries, and the distinctions between the Christian and the secular in modern history often are not agreed on.

The first part of the preceding definition emphasizes the realm over which Christ reigns with power. This realm often is broadened to include the secular and the sacred, and it points toward the future in a powerful way, predicting that the secular will be overcome by the sacred. The second part of the definition focuses on the body of believers who are committed to God's rule and live as a body of the redeemed in the present. This emphasis is more temporal for those who live in the kingdom, and it involves a struggle against the secular world, which seeks to establish a kingdom of its own.

The approach taken in this book focuses on the second of these two emphases. The differences between the two worlds and the responsibilities of believers as citizens of the kingdom of God in economic matters are our main concerns. A corollary concern is that contemporary evangelicals have lost the distinction between the two kingdoms in economic life.

The Characteristics of the Kingdom

It is appropriate to review some prominent characteristics that will identify the kingdom of God in our time. First, the story of Nicodemus hints at the radical nature of the calling into the kingdom. Jesus comments that "no one can see the kingdom of God unless he is born again" (John 3:3). For Nicodemus, who was taught the mindset of the Pharisees, only a new orientation, a new mindset, a new world view, could help him see the kingdom. The change is so dramatic that it requires a new history for mind and heart.

The new birth of which Jesus spoke is equally important today because of the secular mindset that is so pervasive in our time. Only a new world view can free one from the power of the world's mold. Therefore, a primary requirement for the kingdom of God today is a new birth of the mind and heart that will foster a careful approach to secular ideals and values.

A second characteristic of the kingdom is illustrated in the parable of the sower in Matthew 13, where Jesus indicates that citizenship in God's kingdom is given only to those who overcome the significant odds of temptation, superficial commitment, and attachment to the secular preoccupations of success and security. Only those who remain good soil and bear fruit are worthy of the kingdom.

> Listen then to what the parable of the sower means: When anyone hears the message about the kingdom and does not understand it, the evil one comes and snatches away what was sown in his heart. This is the seed sown along the path. The one who received the seed that fell on rocky places is the man who hears the word and at once receives it with joy. But since he has no root, he lasts only a short time. When trouble or persecution comes because of the word, he quickly falls away. The one who received the seed that fell among the thorns is the man who hears the word, but the worries of this life and the deceitfulness of wealth choke it, making it unfruitful. But the one who received the seed that fell on good soil is the man who hears the word and understands it. He produces a crop, yielding a hundred, sixty or thirty times what was sown. [Matt. 13:18–23]

A third characteristic of the kingdom is that its citizens exist in society alongside citizens of the secular kingdom. They are not isolated or separate from the world geographically. The parable of the wheat and tares in Matthew 13:24–30 indicates that, though the two kingdoms are clearly distinguishable, they coexist in society. Christians are in the world but not of the world (John 17:11, 14, 16). What it means to be not of the world is one of the more ignored themes in Scripture because contemporary Christianity in the west enjoys life in the world. On this topic Ronald J. Sider wrote:

> Two Biblical texts serve well to underline my thesis. The first is Matthew 7:13, "Enter by the narrow gate for the gate is wide and the way is easy, that leads to destruction and those who enter by it are many." And the second is Romans 12:1, 2, "I appeal to you therefore, siblings, by the mercies of God, to present your bodies as a living sacrifice, holy and acceptable to God, which is your spiritual worship. Do not be conformed to this world but be transformed

by the renewal of your mind, that you may prove what is the will of God, what is good and acceptable and perfect."

Too many Christian colleges have forgotten the very sharp contrast the New Testament draws between the church and the world. Jesus stated bluntly that the world "hates me because I testify of it that its works are evil" (John 7:7). . . .

The church and the world are in deadly conflict. Many Christian colleges refuse to accept the depth and breadth of that conflict. Yet the fundamental incompatibility between the world and Jesus' new community is so great that I John says we cannot love the world and the Father at the same time: "Do not love the world or the things of the world. If you love the world, the love for the Father is not in you. For all that is in the world, the lust of the flesh, and the lust of the eyes and the pride of life, is not of the Father but is of the world" (I John 2:15–16).[2]

Although Sider's message is directed to the Christian college, it points out that the true kingdom of God contrasts dramatically with the secular kingdom in which it lives. One may suggest that the Judaic-Christian influence on western culture and the enlightenment view of man have reduced the hostility of society toward the kingdom of God, but it takes considerable imagination to believe that the behavior of the secular kingdom has become more compatible with the teachings of Jesus.

Matthew 13:44–48 suggests that the kingdom of heaven is worth more to the believer than all the secular kingdom has to offer. At Jesus' trial he made it very clear that the source of his kingdom is different from the secular kingdom's and that his kingdom therefore operates by different behavioral norms. "My kingdom is not of this world. If it were, my servants would fight to prevent my arrest by the Jews. But now my kingdom is from another place" (John 18:36).

The characteristics of the kingdom listed so far are significant, but they do not give clear behavioral direction to citizens of the kingdom. On issues of behavioral norms, ambiguity occurs in the Christian experience. This is particularly true in economic life, where Christians reach virtually no consensus on norms for economic behavior.

---

2. Ronald J. Sider, "The Christian College: Beachhead or Bullwork?" *The Other Side,* vol. 14 (August 1978): 18–19.

Perhaps an explanation for the lack of consensus among believers on economic concerns is that much of the biblical content on economic behavior appears obscure or idealistic. Believers often feel as if they must fall back on secular norms as guidelines for economic behavior. The Bible's answers just don't seem applicable. At this point two additional significant and related characteristics of the kingdom of God must be examined in order to develop a strategy for kingdom activity.

First, those who share in the fellowship of faith have a special responsibility to discern right and wrong in many controversial matters. The fact that wisdom is imparted through the group, not through individuals alone, is a prominent theme in the New Testament. This is not to suggest that the word from the Lord cannot come to individuals. It merely recognizes that in many difficult and controversial issues there are ambiguities. In such cases, group discernment and discipling are necessary. Even when an individual claims to have a word from the Lord, the validity of his claim frequently is tested by the group, which has a broader base of spiritual gifts.

The effectiveness of the group in decision making and ministry derives from the way in which God has endowed the community of faith with an assortment of gifts. The body of believers is compared in Scripture with the human body. Individuals complement and support each other with their respective gifts (1 Cor. 10:17; Rom. 12:5). These gifts are given for the common good and work together to help the body discern its direction with wisdom. Sharing, rejoicing, weeping, and praying with each other, as a closely knit family would do, are also essential characteristics of Christians (Rom. 12:10–13). Perhaps 1 Corinthians 13 is the key to the success of the body of believers in the world. If the church can express *agapē* love within itself in the manner described in this passage, then the other characteristics of the kingdom will become by-products of that expression and the discerning function of the church will be practiced more faithfully.

Second, because believers have been bonded together with complementary gifts that help them to discern what should be done, they also are charged with the responsibility to disciple each other so that they can remain faithful to their calling. The care with which Jesus built the church indicates how important the body of believers was to him. The work of discipling was one task to which

he paid special attention. His response when Peter affirmed that
Jesus was the Christ (Matt. 16:16) indicates that the church, as a
body of believers, was to play an important role in discipling those
who were committed to the kingdom of God. An example of how
this discipling, or "binding and loosing," process is to function
appears in Matthew 18:15–20. In this case a person is instructed
to resolve conflict by moving progressively toward more involvement with fellow church people until a solution is found. The
power of the church to "bind and loose" on matters where discipling is indicated is substantial.

Jesus' further statement to Peter in Matthew 16:17–19 helps to
clarify this issue. D. A. Carson, in *The Expositor's Bible Commentary,* points out that the keys to the kingdom and the responsibilities of binding and loosing spoken of in these verses belong to
the committed believers who are mainstream in the secular
world.

> In full Christian perspective the kingdom will be consummated in
> sudden, apocalyptic fashion at the Parousia, when God's actions are
> final and quite independent of human means. But now the keys of
> the kingdom are confided to men. They must proclaim the Good
> News, forbid entrance, urge conversion. They constitute a small
> minority in a big world: their mission will be to function as the
> eschatological *ekklesia,* the people of God Jesus is building within
> this world. Inevitably the assignment involves them in using the
> keys to bind and loose. These verses are therefore the result of the
> partially realized and one day to be consummated eschatology im-
> plicit in the N[ew] T[estament].[3]

The point of this interpretation is that, although Peter did play a
special role in church history, the body of believers as a called-out
church has responsibility to use the keys of the kingdom. Carson
continues:

> Confirmation that this is the way 16:19 is to be taken comes at
> 18:18. If the church, Messiah's eschatological people already
> gathered now, has to exercise the ministry of the keys, if it must
> bind and loose, then clearly one aspect of that will be the discipline

---

3. D. A. Carson, "Matthew," in *The Expositor's Bible Commentary* ed. Frank
E. Gaebelein, 12 vols. (Grand Rapids: Zondervan, 1984), 8:373.

of those who profess to constitute it. Thus the two passages are tightly joined: 18:18 is a special application of 16:19. Again, if we may judge from Paul's ministry, this discipline is a special function of apostles, but also of elders and even of the whole church (1 Cor 5:1–13; 2 Cor 13:10; Titus 2:15; 3:10–11)—an inescapable part of following Jesus during this age of the inaugurated kingdom and of the proleptic gathering of Messiah's people. The church of Jesus Christ is more than an audience. . . . The continuity depends as much on discipline as on truth. Indeed, faithful promulgation of the latter both entails and presupposes the former.[4]

Howard A. Snyder, in *The Community of the King,* also speaks of the church as the body that gives substance to the kingdom of God in our time. "The Kingdom of God has not fully come but it is coming. Its full establishment awaits the return of Christ. But through the life and work of God's people—the Church—it continues to expand and grow. And understanding the Kingdom is closely bound up with understanding the Church."[5]

The Contrast of the Kingdoms

Thus, to summarize, the kingdom of God, as personified in the community of faith, contrasts sharply with the secular kingdom in which that community lives. Active participation in it is required of the Christian, and the community's sincere efforts to find truth and encourage people to practice it will be rewarded if members are committed enough to love each other and work together as a body.

This two-kingdom model in no way denies the universality of God's domain. It merely recognizes that part of that domain although under his control has not committed itself to his highest purpose. Further, the kingdom of God is not fully here because people are frail and come short of God's ideal even in their best moments. Yet, believers work toward the ideals and, with God's help, are able to have glimpses of how God wants the redeemed to live.

---

4. Ibid., p. 374.
5. Howard A. Snyder, *The Community of the King* (Downers Grove: Inter-Varsity, 1977), p. 31.

Figure 3
The Two Kingdoms

Kingdom of God
Inhabited by fallen people
  who by God's grace are made
  whole and bear fruit
Clearly distinguished
  from secular society
Has a unique source (not
  from this world)
Has the power of discerning
  right and wrong in ambiguous
  areas
Functions as a community of
  interrelated parts
Temporal and eternal

A

Kingdom of This World
Inhabited by fallen
  people who do not
  know God
Self-centered,
  seeking to gratify
  desires
Right and wrong
  determined by the
  influential and
  powerful people
Functions in an
  atomistic,
  individualistic mode
Temporal

B

C

It may be helpful at this point to represent the preceding discussion schematically (see fig. 3). The secular kingdom in this case relates to the western market capitalistic orientation. The two kingdoms are depicted as mutually exclusive because of the differences in their origin, goals, and philosophical orientation. Obvious areas of meaningful overlap will be discussed later, but for now the differences are our primary concern.

From figure 3, three areas of discussion can be identified. The first concern is with the relationships within the kingdom of God. These relationships are labeled A in the figure. Scripture has much to say about the interactions among believers in all areas of life, but only the economic relationships will be explored in the following chapters.

Letter B identifies relationships in secular society. In the economic area these vary depending on the particular economic system accepted by a given society. As a rule, these relationships serve the interests of whatever social unit that secular society considers most important. In some cases, as in western capitalism, the basic social unit is the individual; in other cases the state is foremost. Scripture says very little about these relationships except for a few reality statements about the secular kingdom's economic situation.

Letter C stands for the interkingdom relationships. How does the Christian relate to the economic institutions of the secular

Figure 4
Comparison of the Kingdoms

Kingdom of God (A)		Kingdom of This World (B)
The total welfare of people	key goal	Individual freedom symbolized in right of property
Christian love	motivating force to reach goal	Self-interest with some moral restraints
Cooperation	means to goal	Competition
Need-based voluntary sharing	allocative device	Auction price system
Church involvement in norm setting and disciplining	regulator or guide over process	Limited government

environment? This question will be addressed in chapter 12 following closer examination of the intrakingdom relationships depicted in A and B.

Figure 3 can be a useful framework for further discussion because there can be a great deal of confusion in the interpretation of biblical passages if those that refer to one set of relationships are applied to another. For example, the type of sharing expected of believers cannot be expected of unbelievers, who are not committed to the discipline of a community of faith. Likewise, it is unlikely that the secular world can operate with the economic norms the church should practice.

The two-kingdom model becomes more meaningful when realistically illustrated. Using democratic capitalism as representative of a given secular system, and the New Testament teachings as representative of the qualities of the kingdom of God, one can draw a series of contrasts. Figure 4 depicts the economic subset of figure 3. Oversimplification can occur easily in this kind of description of the two systems. However, there is enough contrast between them to make this dichotomy a useful tool for analysis.

Although there are, perhaps, as many different sets of secular economic characteristics as there are systems, the constant in the discussion is that secular systems all contrast sharply with the qualities of the kingdom of God. Thus the Christian will always feel a tension in economic behavior. Indeed, he should always feel like a pilgrim and a stranger when immersed in the institutions of the secular world. However, for the most part, western Christians do not feel that way. Many believe that a little fine tuning of secular economic relationships can make them consistent with kingdom-of-God norms.

The Community of Faith and Kingdom Practice

It may be helpful to consider a question that frequently arises at this point: What types of organizations can be expected to operate with kingdom-of-God norms? Are Christian colleges, parachurch organizations, and large congregations expected to function with the kingdom-of-God relationships? Probably not. Most of these entities are too large to have meaningful discipling and accountability relationships. In a college of several thousand people, it may be impractical to base salaries on need. However, every believer should be part of some community of faith that seeks to practice kingdom-of-God values in a caring environment with discipling and accountability. Self-actualization and security for persons and their families should be part of the setting where the kingdom of God is becoming a reality.

The institutional framework most helpful in meeting these characteristics seems to have the following qualities:

1. The community of faith must be small enough that all members can share in a committed and caring way with each other (perhaps five to ten families).
2. Each community of faith should be part of a larger body that can offer general counsel and support and perhaps be a context for worship. This may be a larger congregation or a conference body that offers programs that a small group cannot provide. Christian education, mission outreach programs, publishing capability, and help in determining general behavioral norms are functions that the small community of faith might seek from the larger congregation or district group.

3. A denominational tie is valuable for a worldwide witness and a theological and historical heritage. Internationalizing the Christian vision is essential to prevent a community of faith from becoming ingrown and provincial.

Thus the community of faith will most likely be a small subset of a larger congregation that has denominational ties. The collection of all believers everywhere constitutes the whole church that is attempting to help practice the ideals God gives his people. The model of those ideals toward which the church is striving is the kingdom of God, a reality that is breaking through even now.

Two things remain to be done in fleshing out kingdom-of-God relationships. First, we must solve the hermeneutical problem of how the economist of a modern capitalist society should read biblical literature, which is totally precapitalist in orientation. Second, we need to paint a picture of what some intrakingdom-of-God relationships might look like in our time.

Discussion Questions

1. Do you think that this two-kingdom approach to the application of biblical principles underestimates the potential for good of the secular world?
2. This two-kingdom approach implies that believers have a higher calling and different behavioral expectations for themselves than for nonbelievers. Do you believe this is appropriate? If so, what implications might this have for social and political behavior as well as economic practice?
3. Can you articulate the arguments of those like George Gilder, in *Wealth and Poverty,* and Michael Novak, in *The Spirit of Democratic Capitalism,* who suggest that the Christian tradition and market capitalism share the same values?

5

Reading the Bible
with Modern Glasses

From our perspective, people in Bible times held two very strange ideas about economic activity. First, they thought there were only so many goods and services available to be distributed to the people. Increasing the economic pie by expanding productivity over time was not part of their thinking. Second, they thought this constant pie of production was fixed permanently at roughly an amount equal to what it took to keep the population alive and well but not expanding. In other words, life was destined to be a subsistence, steady-state existence.

There was natural productivity in nature, to be sure. Seeds grew into plants with many seeds, and people could more than replace themselves with large families, as could animals. But the trend was not toward growth, because natural productivity barely kept ahead of subsistence needs. Crops were consumed as fast as they were produced; death rates and birth rates were similar from year to year; famine, plague, and war constantly threatened the survival of the human race.

Nevertheless, prosperity is mentioned frequently in Scripture. Many refer to the Old Testament passages where obedience led to plenty (Deut. 8:12–20; 1 Kings 10). Others see economic growth assumed in the teachings of Paul or the parables of Jesus (Eph. 4:28; Luke 12:13–21). However, there is a difference between the ability to work hard, produce, and even prosper for a time and the concept that higher and higher living standards will prevail because of perpetual technology-driven growth. The ancient world saw prosperity as an unusual favor from God or the gods: a return for obedience that could be quickly lost. In the mind of the western capitalist, growth comes from the productivity of capital and high savings rates and is expected as the normal pattern. In the ancient world God gives the increase, in the modern world the increase comes as people fit into the normal pattern of how the world works. The ancient view was confirmed by the perpetually low standard of living experienced by the average citizen of the time. The modern view is confirmed by the constant increase in the average standard of living of successive generations over several centuries.

From the earliest estimates to the fifteenth century, the size of the earth's population increased only slightly by modern standards, and the standard of living was rarely very far above subsistence. In fact, it was news when someone prospered for a time. In Old Testament times Jacob returned to his homeland from Laban's town a wealthy person, but later he became dependent on Egypt's bounty for subsistence. In this case as in the cases of Abraham and others, wealth was mainly in the form of cattle, sheep, and goats. Precious metal was a component of wealth, but it was usually in the form of jewelry of some kind. Not until the seventh century B.C. did coins appear as a medium of exchange or store of value. The earliest known Hebrew coin was minted in Judah in the fourth century B.C.[1] Whatever the form of wealth, it was seen not as a ticket to perpetual prosperity but as a reprieve from the hardships of nature or a display of power and influence.

The display of wealth by the Hebrew kings was evidence of their power and influence in domestic and foreign relationships, but the prophets also viewed it as a cause of poverty in the land. One author describes precapitalist wealth as follows:

> Wealth appears in such forms as goods or services devoted to luxury consumption, to the maintenance and deployment of armed force, to religious edifices, or simply to display. Wealth thereby takes on the properties of "use values," to use the term that Marx adopts from Adam Smith and Aristotle, including not least the use value of expressing the might and grandeur of rulership itself.

---

1. Pat Alexander, ed., *Lion Encyclopedia of the Bible,* revised ed. (Batavia, Ill.: Lion, 1986), p. 241.

Conspicuously absent from these means of utilizing wealth is its application for a purpose central to, and indeed constitutive of, capitalism. This is the use of wealth in various concrete forms, not as an end in itself, but as a means for gathering more wealth. The closest analogue to this in ancient kingdoms, is the employment of military or religious or regal institutions and equipages, not merely as symbols of power and prestige desired for their own sakes but as instruments for military, religious, or dynastic expansion.[2]

The important part of all of this discussion is that precapitalist societies had no understanding of the economic-growth-and-prosperity mentality of the twentieth-century capitalist. Conversely, the modern capitalist finds it difficult to step into the shoes of the first-century farmer or craftsman. Consequently we read into Scripture things that are not there and we miss some of the lessons that are being taught.

This gulf of misunderstanding has contributed much to a widespread misreading of biblical texts on wealth. The thesis of this chapter is that the biblical writers had little if any understanding of productive capital as a form of wealth; Scripture therefore is silent on that very recent form of wealth.[3] Instead, wealth was viewed as hoarded future consumption that contributed nothing to future production.

The biblical world saw three uses for income. First, everyone used part of present income for present consumption. Maintaining a certain standard of living was an important claim on income. Second, part of income went to tithes and offerings. Third,

---

2. Robert L. Heilbroner, *The Nature and Logic of Capitalism* (New York: W. W. Norton, 1985), pp. 34–35.

3. The term *productive capital* may be confusing to some. For those who are not familiar with the way economists use this concept, the term *productive machinery* would be a helpful substitute throughout this chapter. When a typewriter replaced a pencil the production of the writer increased dramatically. Likewise, the computer has multiplied the output of the writer even more. The same process of output increase occurred when a shovel replaced hands and a backhoe replaced the shovel. Inert machinery has the same kind of power that a grain of wheat has, although that was not recognized until relatively recently in history. However, just like the planted grain of wheat, the machine uses resources that might have been consumed instead. Thus foregone consumption is required for machine production just as some bread is foregone now so that more bread can be made in the future.

people saved for future consumption. This last category was particularly difficult to justify because, in a world where subsistence living was common, there were always poor people whose income had fallen below their basic needs.

The statement, "the poor you always have with you," can best be understood in light of this static subsistence type of thinking. It would be incorrect to assume that the same statement must apply to a machine-oriented, growth economy that is above subsistence level in per capita income.

It is also important to recognize that this no growth subsistence orientation to economic life leads naturally to strong admonitions against accumulated wealth and to a concentrated focus on income distribution questions rather than production questions. If accumulated wealth was primarily a storing process for future consumption while others were starving, it is not surprising that so many biblical writers clearly spoke against accumulated wealth and emphasized sharing with the poor.

Jesus' parable in Luke 12:13–21 illustrates this thinking well. A farmer with large crops built bigger barns to house his harvest for future consumption. Apparently his savings helped no one in the present. Jesus condemned this practice of securing one's future rather than giving to the poor as sinful and foolish. Immediately after telling this parable, Christ taught about curbing both consumption and savings, concluding in verse 33 by urging his listeners to divest of their hoarded savings by giving to the poor. This directive fits well with the notion that earthly things decay, rust, and become depleted rather than expand, reproduce, and lead to growth for the good of society.

The principle that comes through again and again is that it is wrong to secure your future materially while others are starving. Wealth in Bible times was little more than hoarded resources that prevented others from consuming. It added nothing to future production. Since the pie of production was considered fixed near subsistence, accumulated wealth practically guaranteed that some people would be poor.[4]

---

4. There is one story in Scripture where resources were stored for future consumption and the practice is applauded. Joseph stored seven years of consumption goods in Egypt for use during the coming famine. This case is an unusual one in which God provided special foresight and was working out a special purpose in history by Joseph's actions. In contrast to this story is the

The task for believers today is to relate productive-capital-oriented accumulated wealth to biblical texts directed toward hoarded wealth. Two elements of this task are important. First, we must understand the nature of productive capital and prove that productive capital was not part of the biblical understanding. Second, we must develop the implications of this analysis for a modern understanding of the anti-wealth passages of Scripture.

Viewing Wealth as Productive Capital Is a New Idea

The idea that inventions and creations of people could multiply the output of goods and services, resulting in persistent economic growth and an elevated standard of living, is quite new. Not until after A.D 1000 did capital inventions and innovative processes begin to expand production in ways that caused some to think of continued growth as a possibility. Between A.D. 1000 and 1500 the three-field system dramatically increased agricultural output; the four-wheeled wagon was invented; horses replaced oxen as field animals, reducing the number of people required for field work; and the enclosure movement of land ownership transformed common property into private property. These innovations brought amazing results, but they were only a foretaste of the increased output that would come in the industrial revolution of the eighteenth century.[5] The unleashing of productive forces in that century forever changed the way people think about resources and production.

The change was not just technical. Attitudes toward growth, acquisition, education, and social order changed radically. The following quote represents not only medieval thought but also thinking that had prevailed for centuries before.

> Any account of medieval social and economic thought must also stress the great disdain with which people viewed trade and commerce and the commercial spirit. The medieval way of life was

case in the wilderness; any storing of manna for future consumption was sinful. This is again a special case of God working out a specific objective. It would be inaccurate to teach against future consumption solely on the basis of the wilderness example, just as it would be wrong to teach a positive view of hoarding on the basis of Joseph's case. The entire scope of biblical teaching must be considered before generalizations are helpful.

5. E. K. Hunt, *Property and Prophets: The Evolution of Economic Institutions and Ideologies,* 4th ed. (Cambridge: Harper and Row, 1981), p. 13.

based on custom and tradition; its viability depended on the acceptance by the members of society of that tradition and their place within it. Where the capitalist commercial ethic prevails, greed, selfishness, covetousness, and the desire to better oneself materially or socially are accepted by most people as innate qualities. Yet they were uniformly denounced and reviled in the Middle Ages. The serfs (and sometimes the lower nobility) tended to be dissatisfied with the traditions and customs of medieval society and thus threatened the stability of the feudal system. It is not surprising, therefore, to find pervasive moral sanctions designed to repress or to mitigate the effects of these motives.[6]

This mindset, which the Christian church of that time reinforced, was completely altered by the events of the centuries that followed. Wealth accumulation became not only appropriate but laudatory. Trade and commerce became respectable and were seen as beneficial to everyone. Education—or human capital, as economists call it—shifted from teaching how to reproduce the past to teaching that the future must be different and better. The entire world view changed so that growth and the prospect of plenty replaced the static, no-growth subsistence life of earlier times. The productivity of machinery and ideas brought the prospect of a brighter future and salvation from a life of subsistence. No biblical writer could have discussed the ethical implications of capital productivity with any credibility because it would have been so foreign to his audience.

Some people argue, because of the stories of rapid wealth accumulation and references to interest returns on savings, that biblical writers understood capital productivity. However, wealth accumulations described in the Bible typically came from sporadic increases in natural productivity, not from machine productivity. The seven years of feast and seven years of famine in Egypt during the time of Joseph exemplify how wealth was viewed in biblical times. Land and cattle could bring amazing increases on occasion, but eventual famine and decline were inevitable. Over time there was no prospect for sustained economic growth for society.

The passages on interest are particularly interesting. The parable of the talents (Matt. 25:14–30) often is used to argue that

6. Ibid., p. 9.

productive capital was a part of New Testament thinking. A strong case can be made against that view. Interest returns on loans derive from four sources in the modern world: (1) The productivity of capital means that a dollar of consumption foregone today will buy a tool that may return a dollar and a half tomorrow. Part of the fifty-cent increase is shared with the lender as interest. (2) Someone who needs money for present consumption is willing to promise a richer person some interest incentive to lend him money. Wherever present consumption is preferred to future consumption it bears a cost. Economists call this the *time-preference* reason for interest. (3) There is always a risk involved in lending money or anything else of value. It might not be returned, or might not be returned in full. The debtor might die, or his business enterprise might fail, or any number of other unforeseen problems might make it impossible for him to repay the loan. Lenders try to reduce this risk by charging interest on loans so that loans that are paid off, including interest, make up for those that are not. (4) In an economy with an expanding money supply, inflation frequently reduces the purchasing power of money. This means that repayment for loans comes in money of lower value than the money initially loaned. Lenders factor their inflation forecasts into their interest rates.

All four of these factors, then, affect interest rates, but any one of them is sufficient incentive to charge interest on a loan. In Bible times it was the time-preference factor that most affected interest rates. Old Testament law, however, argued that this type of interest was not ethical. In the context of the times it is easy to see why interest was considered wrong. If the loan were used for some needy person's consumption, it should either be given as charity or at least kept on the books as an interest-free loan in hopes of more prosperous times for the debtor. To extract a return from the poor was considered inhumane. Even today, when people give money to poor people who need help for basic living, it is not customary to charge interest. Thus welfare payments by the state require neither interest nor repayment. The interest in the parable of the talents could be seen merely as return on consumption loans rather than as proof of a productive-capital concept in the ancient world. In short, the mention of interest in Scripture is not proof that a concept of production capital existed at that time.

The key idea to keep in mind when reading the biblical passages is that first-century people had no developed understanding of savings as productive capital or tools that could increase production later. Instead, they saw saving as hoarding, which amounted to selfish behavior when others did not have enough for immediate consumption. Had the farmer in Luke 12 set aside some of his output to create better seed or a new tool of production so that he could double his output in the following year, Christ might have praised him for effective planning toward the goal of solving hunger in society.

To summarize, wealth, to New Testament writers, was basically an accumulation of goods that put more consumption power into the hands of the wealthy few at the expense of the working majority. The accumulations of the rich did not enhance productive capacity in future years or create jobs for anyone. Instead, they fostered greater disparities of life style in society. Wealth was the vehicle to more luxurious living.

It is from this orientation that the New Testament consistently condemns riches and wealth. To become rich was automatically to be more concerned for self than for others, since it meant securing one's own future before caring about current economic suffering. How could such an individual possibly be a participant in the kingdom of God that Jesus was initiating? Only through a miracle of God, if at all (Matt. 19:24, 26; Luke 18:24–25, 27).

Not only did accumulating wealth contradict kingdom principles, but also the preoccupation with wealth was a rich person's constant temptation. "No servant can serve two masters. Either he will hate the one and love the other, or he will be devoted to the one and despise the other. You cannot serve both God and Money" (Luke 16:13). To run an earthly empire while being a disciple in God's kingdom was viewed as a basic contradiction by Jesus and the New Testament writers.

More could be made of this teaching. One way of interpreting the passages concerned with wealth is to view them as assuming that preoccupation with wealth is inevitable for the rich unless they give it away in acts of charity. At the very least, the temptations the wealthy face are not easy to overcome, even for the most committed person. Consequently, wealth was condemned in Bible times because it was hoarded and because it posed enormous temptations of idolatry.

It would be inappropriate to downplay the sharp condemnation of wealth in Scripture simply because productive wealth is now more common than hoarded wealth. The danger of idolatry is present in all times. However, it is important to recognize the new category of wealth as one not spoken of in Scripture. In other words, it is inappropriate to condemn a wealthy business person today by using the anti-wealth passages of Scripture if his wealth is accumulated in productive tools for socially desirable output and he successfully resists the temptations of being rich. In the next chapter, we will consider how a believer might defend against the dangers of productive wealth. At this point it is only necessary to distinguish between first-century hoarded wealth and modern productive wealth.

Scripture Condemns Hoarding Wealth

Because accumulated wealth in biblical times was hoarded wealth, rather than productive wealth, it is criticized frequently in Scripture. However, some argue that wealth is not always rebuked in Scripture. Jacob's accumulation and Job's faithfulness amid enormous riches are not subjects for anti-wealth teaching, but neither are they affirmations of wealth, any more than Jacob's deceitfulness in acquiring the birthright is appropriate behavior for gaining a desired end. The Old Testament stories weave together events and teaching in ways that can be sorted out only by an appeal to the prominent themes of Scripture that occur throughout the entire text. Concern for lavish wealth is one of those themes because there was a perception that one person's wealth was detrimental, not beneficial, to the masses. Passages that indicate otherwise are usually historical narrative rather than normative teaching.

A chart showing the differences in income use by the ancient and modern worlds appears in figure 5. The significant difference between the two orientations is that productive investment appears in the center column but not in the left column. Discerning the meaning of that difference is an important part of the next chapter, but this chapter has presented the view that productive wealth may be appropriate to hold since it generates increasing future production for society to consume.

Figure 5
Biblical Approaches to Ancient
and Modern Uses of Wealth

Ancient	Modern	Biblical Approach
Consumption	Consumption	Modest living taught in Scripture
Charity	Charity	Required of believers
Hoarded future consumption	Hoarded future consumption	Condemned by Scripture
	Productive capital	Not treated specifically in Scripture

To summarize, because the biblical writers did not live in a world that emphasized capital tools of production, and because their world was basically a no-growth, steady-state environment, Scripture does not offer a perspective on accumulated wealth in the form of capital goods. This perspective is left for believers to develop as the world continues to move into a capital-oriented economy. Sadly, believers have not pursued this task carefully, so business people today are criticized by many believers who use Scripture as if they lived in a first-century world. Also, the business person and those sympathetic to the business community frequently see no alternative but to seek scriptural texts, usually in the wisdom literature of the Old Testament, as counterevidence that the anti-wealth tone in Scripture is really not there. Neither of these improper approaches has been helpful to the community of faith.

The next chapter will attempt to describe how believers should relate to one another on economic matters in a way that will be biblically sound and yet take into account the very different economic world in which we live. The dangers of accumulated wealth are still very real, and the believer today must not take them lightly—even if the accumulation is in productive wealth.

Discussion Questions

1. This chapter argues that wealth in the form of productive investment is not condemned in Scripture because it did not

exist then as it does today. Can you think of any Bible passages that might relate to productive investment as we perceive it?

2. If our economy today were a constant-sum environment like
   the biblical people understood their world to be, would we
   have different views on economic justice? If so, how might
   our thinking about economic distribution change?

6

A Radical Economic Model for Today

It should be clear now that the complicated, machine-oriented economy in which we live has made the task of interpreting Scripture more difficult. The categories of income use listed in the last chapter provide an agenda for discussion. In the ancient world, consumption, charity, and hoarding were the categories deemed relevant. Hoarding was considered sinful because in a constant-sum economy that was at or near subsistence, any hoarding was viewed as taking from others what they needed at the moment for survival.

The New and Old Testament critique of riches is not focused on the earning of income but on its misuse. The misuse could be in the form of either hoarding or consumption. A typical charge to the high-income earner is found in 1 Timothy 6:17–19: "Command those who are rich in this present world not to be arrogant nor to put their hope in wealth, which is so uncertain, but to put their hope in God, who richly provides us with everything for our enjoyment. Command them to do good, to be rich in good deeds, and to be generous and willing to share."

Some have used this passage to justify high consumption because God "provides us with everything for our enjoyment." We can see the fallacy of this interpretation by beginning at verse 3 rather than at verse 17. In these verses Timothy critiques contentious people "of corrupt mind, who have been robbed of the truth and who think that godliness is a means to financial gain.

But godliness with contentment is great gain. For we brought nothing into the world, and we can take nothing out of it. But if we have food and clothing we will be content with that" (1 Tim. 6:5–8). If consumption was to be modest and hoarding was wrong, then that left only charity as an outlet for high earnings. Tithing is not highlighted in the New Testament because, after a modest living was secured, the rest belonged to the Lord as charity. The Old Testament notion of offerings above a tithe amounts to a similar teaching.

The term *contentment* was used in the Greek philosophical sense to mean an ideal situation where no aid or support is needed. In 2 Corinthians 9:8, the only other place it is used in the New Testament, contentment relates to the necessities of life. This passage is not an attack on rich people but it is a statement that God values modest living.

Another example of this concern is found in Luke 16:19–31. Here Jesus tells of the nameless rich man who lived in luxury while Lazarus, a beggar, lay at his gate. The implication is strong that the rich man's unwillingness to redistribute some of his income to Lazarus was a factor in his damnation. This theme is consistent with Jesus' commentary on the rich young ruler in Matthew 19:24 and with other teachings, including the behavior of the early church recorded in the Book of Acts.

Indeed, in a context devoid of productive capital the biblical teaching makes logical sense. The prophets' vicious criticism of accumulated wealth and the stinging charges against riches in the New Testament are not overstatements or utopian, egalitarian dreaming. Rather they were legitimate demands from a God who cared about income distribution enough to challenge the rich to live modestly and give mightily. The criticism is not against the high income that some apparently had, but rather against how much they consumed and how little they gave away.

When one moves to the modern world, things become more complicated because of the additional category to which income can be allocated. Productive investment now becomes another way to use income. As discussed before, this area is not mentioned in Scripture; neither was it a prominent concern in the history of the church until relatively recently, when machines became important in the production process. Thus believers must use careful discernment to allocate their income effectively. The task is more difficult than it was in the first century because now there are three legitimate uses for money: hoarding, or nonproductive investment as it might be called, is still as wrong as it was in the ancient world; that leaves consumption, charity, and productive investment.

The fact that the church has said very little about how believers should handle financial matters is a tragedy that needs correcting. Typically the only principle articulated is that believers should give at least 10 percent of their income to charity, but beyond that the believer is on his own. Investment and consumption are matters for private consideration. Market price signals and individual preferences alone guide decision making. Believers as a group usually do not become involved in the moral dilemmas of the decision process. In fact, financial secrecy is thought a virtue. Presumably, too much information only creates gossip, jealousy, and dissension. Perhaps this is evidence of how the church has accepted secular values in economic matters.

Striving for Responsibility

What follows is a discussion of how believers might become more responsible in the categories of income generation, consumption, charity, and productive investment. In other words, what should the relationships labeled A in chapter 4 look like in a church that wants to be faithful, both individually and collectively, in economic matters?

Choices in Income Generation

Believers are employed in a wide variety of secular and Christian organizations. One might judge her usefulness to society by the salary level she can command. Generally, the higher her pay the more valuable her contribution, but it is clear that the value of the contribution is measured by secular standards. For example, a brewmaster might make more money than a nurse, but a believer will consider other matters before becoming a brewmaster. Nearly every Christian job seeker needs wider input than just salary figures. This is where the community of believers can help in discerning a person's gifts and evaluating the moral issues that surround a particular job offer. When I came out of graduate school, the body of believers in my church convinced me that I could serve God better in a job that offered little more than half what the highest-alternative position offered. I knew they were right, but without them I probably would have made a different choice.

Questions of gift discernment among believers must be generalized beyond simply staffing Sunday school and church outreach programs. When a community of believers gives its blessing to a member's job, additional involvement in economic issues becomes less difficult. It must be emphasized that the size of one's income is neither the key concern nor a measure of one's worth or influence in the church. Some may earn very high pay and receive the blessing of the believers, who recognize the reward that a market brings to highly skilled people. Others may value leisure more and willingly make the trade-offs required to follow their preferences. The ramifications of this option should be discussed in community as well. In short, the community of faith must be more involved in work and leisure choices and in the concerns that come to people as they live out their choices.

Choices in Consumption

The first claim on family income is usually consumption. People generally determine the standard of living that they will maintain and then protect it as carefully as possible. One component of the standard of living is the growth rate one seeks in his life style. How are the consumption standards set? What values influence those standards and the plans for future consumption? The answers to these questions are fairly easy to find in the secular world. In general, income levels determine consumption standards and the hope is for as rapid growth as possible. Perpetual growth is a dominant western value.

There is little evidence that Christians follow a different pattern, except for those who choose simple living and low pay in order to enter special areas of Christian service. Perhaps the area of consumption is the most serious blind spot contemporary Christians have in the exercise of their faith. There are several reasons for this. First, any dollar spent on consumption is unavailable for charity or productive investment. Second, people are less inclined to relate to those who have living standards appreciably above their own. Thus, those with substantially above-average life styles limit the range of their ministry. Third, an abundance of things can easily create a feeling of self-sufficiency that tends to crowd out God. Scripture abounds with statements on the risks of high living. Fourth, an abundance of things predisposes one to protect those things in ways that require more expenditures on insurance and crime deterrence. Fifth, luxurious living makes it hard to identify with poor people everywhere.

In view of all this, why is the church so silent on consumption? The answer is complex, but certainly the ambiguities of determining what is luxury, what is need, and when *things* are becoming too important are part of the problem. The common phrase, "Everything is relative," can sidetrack any preacher brave enough to suggest restraint of life style. In fact, everything *is* relative in these matters, and that is the most compelling reason why the community of believers must use its God-given gifts of discernment to enable the Christian to make responsible use of resources. Some suggestions may be helpful, although for many these suggestions will seem more like meddling than preaching.

First, the amount that a typical family spends on itself should be within some carefully conceived range around the average of the community in which it is called to minister. For example, if the average family consumption in the community around a church is twenty-three thousand dollars, then members might try to have consumption patterns within a range of sixteen to thirty thousand dollars. This is not an effort to introduce a legalistic rule but to establish an expectation from which believers deviate only with careful thought, prayer, and the blessing of their community of faith. Some may have good reasons for living above or below this expectation; the community of faith should affirm more extreme life styles for those with special circumstances.

The important point here is that deviations do not occur automatically, out of habit, or because of rapid income changes, but after consideration of issues related to the church's ministry and a particular family's needs. Christian groups often have discovered a new dimension of faith and found the exercise of stewardship easier and more rewarding when members are willing to share and be accountable to each other.

This suggestion appears less radical than at first blush when we realize that living standards are usually set not in a vacuum but relative to some social group. Therefore, it seems important to make the values of the church the reference point for Christians rather than the values of a secular group. Secular norms invariably point to continually higher living standards as evidence of success and importance. If the church articulates no values, then the standards of the world will become the norm for the believer.

One complication of establishing consumption norms like those suggested is that those who fall below the consumption range will need a subsidy from the church. Usually this is done only for those in mission work or church employment or in cases of accident or disaster. In these situations the church evaluates each case on its merits and offers help where it seems appropriate. There is no reason why poorer families in the church should not apply for help in the same manner to have their consumption level brought up to the minimum standard considered appropriate by the community of faith. Although this seems too radical for many, it is far less radical than the communal treasury practice of many intentional communities across the United States and around the world.

Choices in Giving

The next category of income allocation is charity. Since the church has typically preached a 10 percent tithing rule as a minimum for believers, there is less that needs to be said here except to notice that in our modern environment, reduced consumption by the wealthy may not necessarily end up in charity. It may also be directed toward productive investment, which is a legitimate use of income.

One facet of giving, too often overlooked, is the joy that generous sharing brings to the believer. The real blessings of giving are intangible rather than material, although we frequently talk of God's blessings in material terms. Nowhere in the Bible is a lavish standard of living promised to those who share their resources with others. The much abused passage in Matthew 6:33 is perhaps the strongest directive to believers to practice a more explicit economic model of sharing than they presently do. The command to "seek first his kingdom" requires adopting the characteristics described earlier in chapter 4, and the things that will be given are the basic needs of life that God provides for the lilies and the birds. Clearly luxurious consumption is the antithesis of all that this section of the Sermon on the Mount is about.

If material sufficiency, not plenty, is a reward for giving, and if the believer already has his basic needs met, is there a blessing in giving? Certainly! The joy of helping in the cause of the church may be the greatest undertapped renewable resource the world will ever have. That joy is multiplied because giving draws one closer to the programs of the church and its caring, discerning process. Being closer to the church affects one's witness in many ways including, most importantly, how one's children view faith and practice. When the church becomes the focus of one's life, the model being developed here becomes possible and the world can see an exciting way of life that makes concrete what the call to faith is all about. In short, giving puts one's treasure and one's heart in the church.

Because the most obvious expression of the church is the local congregation, it is important to give the majority of one's contribution to the local church rather than to organizations that have far less accountability to their supporters. One whose heart is in the church views the joy and blessings spoken of in Scripture differently from one whose treasure is in the world of material gain and high consumption.

The Problem of Hoarding

Hoarding is difficult to define in modern society. Because of extremely sophisticated and efficient financial markets and fractional reserve banking, most savings are quickly funneled into economic activity. Many will argue that, short of burying valuables in the ground, it is impossible to hoard in a society of efficient markets. Certainly it is true that markets make nearly everything fungible so that a dollar saved somewhere becomes a productive investment elsewhere.

In addition, the idea that services are as important to economic well-being as are goods means that many things that one might do with his income are productive. A valuable painting gives people pleasure as truly as a loom makes clothing for them. Speculating in a market performs the valuable service of spreading

risk that others prefer to avoid. Even burying money in the back
yard has few ill effects on the economy because the Federal Reserve Board expands the money supply if a shortage of loanable
funds occurs. Thus money is available for productive uses anyway.

Some have argued that the enormous amount of rearranging of
assets common in advanced economies is a nonproductive form of
resource use that takes on the characteristics of hoarding. This
case has been argued as follows:

> By any number of measurements including the total amount of
> money, effort, and media attention devoted to each, the ratio of
> asset-rearrangers to asset-enlargers in our economy is running at
> about two to one.
>
> In the last three years some $100 billion of corporate cash re-
> sources have been used to acquire existing corporate assets through
> tender offers. This money could have been spent on new factories
> and other productive uses. . . . Instead of generating future eco-
> nomic expansion, the money circulates among companies like
> stakes in a floating dice game.[1]

Even this assertion is subject to debate. First, it must be shown
that a merger did not in fact increase the productivity of one or
the other parties in the transaction. Second, it is important to
know whether the funds involved in the transaction actually leave
the loanable funds market.

In short, the concept of hoarding in modern times is relevant,
but observing hoarding in practice is virtually impossible. Defining modern hoarding may be the subject of a book that is more
oriented toward finance than this one. Most likely the relevant
framework is one that simply examines investment along a continuum from least productive to most productive rather than com-
paring productive with nonproductive uses of wealth. To some
degree this continuum is part of the discussion of investment that
we will take up shortly.

Before examining productive investment as a category of income use it is important to point out that the effects of hoarding in
today's market-oriented economies are not as damaging as the

---

1. Robert B. Reich, "Pie Slicers *vs.* Pie Enlargers," *The Washington Monthly*
(September 1980): 13–19.

effects of hoarding would have been on a more primitive economy. Today's flexible money supply and efficient capital markets offset hoarding's normally contractionary effects on the larger economy. In other words, the very things that make hoarding hard to define also diminish its negative effect on the economy.

On the other hand, the effect that an accumulation of claims on future income has on one's approach to the Christian life can hardly be overemphasized, whether or not the claims come from productive or nonproductive investment. Both temptations and opportunities for service grow for people with potential for great accumulation. The temptations come in the areas of self-sufficiency, pride, mistrust of the poor, use of power and influence, and the shortage of time available for the pursuit of faith and church life. The opportunities come in some areas of witness, the ability to contribute more to charity, increased organizational and managerial expertise, and the socially desirable output that results if the accumulation is productive. It is a thesis of this book that God never intended people to balance these temptations and opportunities without the help of a caring community of faith. This concept will be pursued later in this chapter.

Choices in Productive Investment

The last category of income use is productive investment. We argued earlier that Scripture gives little direction on this topic, so those who seek to apply the principles of the kingdom of God to their investment behavior must do some careful thinking.

Productive investment can be defined as expenditures that buy tools that will produce goods and services in the future. A tractor, drill press, or factory building will require resources that would otherwise be available for consumption. A dollar spent on a drill press cannot go to feed someone starving today. However, if the drill press is purchased today, the output of the factory may be enough to save more than one person next year. In other words, the business person may be caught in the ethical dilemma of saving one person now or two later. The technological age of our place in history has brought on these time-related kinds of ethical dilemmas.

The business person now has three legitimate outlets for his income. After the consumption level is determined and the charity minimum is given, his remaining income can go toward productive capital investment or additional charity. How this division of surplus is determined is partly a business decision and partly a decision for which he needs guidance from the community of faith. At the very least, he should be able to articulate how the mission of the church and the mission of the business enterprise are complementary and how each will be served by the available funds. When a proprietor chooses to expand the business and give less to the church, he may be making a wise and responsible decision. At the same time, his primary group of believers should be available as a sounding board to check the rationale that led to his decision.

It is unfair for believers to criticize business persons who are wealthy because of extensive assets in productive machinery. It is also inappropriate for business people to build productive empires without any counsel from a community of faith that can help guard against the temptations inherent in the competitive, self-serving economic world. Indeed, the Christian business person needs the church to help discern right from wrong and good from best in certain business decisions, just as much as the church needs the business person for his expertise and his contributions.

The term *business person* is understood in too narrow a fashion most of the time. Participants in the work force invest productively when they take time for job training. Perhaps one of the most widely accepted forms of investment in modern times is the human capital built up in education. Formal education and job training of all kinds are investment activities that nearly everyone engages in at some time, and they represent business decisions that the community of faith should not take lightly. Some churches commission their young people in a special service as they enter new stages of their education, particularly college. This blessing given to an investment by young people should also accompany significant investments by people in other areas of life so that they, too, can proceed with the confidence that their efforts are important to the life of the church, or can alter their plans if sufficient doubts have been raised about the wisdom of a decision.

Involving the Church

This interaction among believers on matters that concern activity in everyday life increases the quality of church life and helps in the believer's effort to meet the temptations and opportunities of the modern economy. It also becomes a powerful witness to a world that finds the individual pursuit of happiness shallow and unfulfilling.

Given the present state of many churches and the prevailing view that one's financial business is a private affair, some may find it hard to imagine how mutual accountability in finances can become part of the Christian agenda. Yet, the more closely a body of believers models the teaching of 1 Corinthians 12 and 13, the more feasible the prospect of mutual accountability in financial matters becomes.

What are some of the advantages and disadvantages of this model for believers today? What are some examples of how the model might work in practice? The advantages could be listed as follows:

1. Key decisions on difficult issues of life style are worked out in community rather than by the prevailing social trend or the individual alone. Individual autonomy in personal consumption and business practice is, to some degree, sacrificed.
2. Large disparities in living standards among believers are carefully examined.
3. Believers can live in the confidence that they have the blessing of the church on their life style.
4. The Lord, through his church, is in control of 100 percent of the resources of his people, not just 10 percent.
5. Society at large, by seeing the Christians, will understand more readily that there is more to life than material things.
6. Questions regarding the appropriateness of various investments and jobs are dealt with collectively so that individual vested interests take second place to an unbiased search for the will of God in the investment decision.
7. The model encourages deeper involvement in the life of the fellowship.

For those who believe that the secular models of resource allocation are appropriate for the church, these advantages may seem
like disadvantages. Many people desire individual autonomy in
economic matters without accountability to other believers. Some
argue that the rules of the economic game and the markets they
make possible are sufficient guidelines for the Christian in economic matters.

The Church: Basic Unit of Economic Decision

The approach presented here questions that understanding because of a fundamental assumption that the basic unit for Christian action is the church, not the individual. That assumption
must be substantiated if the preceding model is to appear credi-
ble.

To say that the community of faith is the basic unit for Christian action means that the church gives its blessing to the behavior of its members in specific ways. It also means that behavior
inconsistent with the expectations of the fellowship of believers is
not overlooked, but dealt with according to biblical principles of
discipline, particularly those spelled out in 2 Timothy 2:23–26.

The need for a committed community of faith as a primary unit
for action is evident from passages like Ephesians 4:11–12, where
the diversity of gifts is discussed: "It was he who gave some to be
apostles, some to be prophets, some to be evangelists, and some to
be pastors and teachers, to prepare God's people for works of
service, so that the body of Christ may be built up. . . ." Clearly,
spiritual wisdom is not complete in any individual, so making
important decisions alone means shortchanging the effectiveness
of the church. To paraphrase the passage in Ephesians, one might
say that if the church does not incorporate its gifts into decision
processes about life style and business practice, it will detract
from the perfecting of the saints, the work of the ministry, and the
edification of the church in those areas of life.

The passages that compare the community of faith to a body
(1 Cor. 12:12–31) and a "building fitly framed together" (Eph.
2:20–22 av) are beautiful illustrations of the interaction in community that is necessary to provide a "habitation of God through
the Spirit" (Eph. 2:22 av). One chapter later, in Ephesians 3:10,
Paul declares that it is through the church that God's plan for

creation is made apparent. "His intent was that now, through the church, the manifold wisdom of God should be made known to the rulers and authorities in the heavenly realms. . . ." In 2 Timothy 2:22 Paul admonished Timothy to avoid evil by immersing himself in the fellowship of Christians: "Flee the evil desires of youth, and pursue righteousness, faith, love and peace, along with those who call on the Lord out of a pure heart." What is clear is that the community of faith is to be far more in the life of believers than an organizational structure for group education, corporate worship, and large help projects.

What is surprising is that the church in twentieth-century America has been able to read the Bible and ignore so many of the dimensions of commitment. Many churches practice little careful discernment. Positive discipline and group norm setting are rarely experienced. Too often individual effort is expended to appropriate the Holy Spirit without the guidance of a committed group of believers, despite the teaching in Ephesians 2:22 and elsewhere. Frequently, institutional structure encumbers the breakthrough of kingdom qualities. The key ingredient required to reverse this situation is found in 1 Corinthians 13, where lists of religious acts are presented as worthless apart from abiding *agapē* love. This love provides content and quality to the commitment needed in the church. Without it, all hope for a dynamic community of faith is lost. The less the people of God appropriate this caring love among themselves, the more unrealistic, idealistic, and improbable the church as a true community of faith will seem.

Criticism is easy, but constructive building is difficult. Some find consolation in the fact that, in the latter part of 1 Corinthians 13, Paul recognizes that perfection will not occur, weaknesses will be present, love will seem far away, and we must wait until the close of history to understand love completely. However, the directive in the first verse of the next chapter is to pursue the way of love eagerly and diligently. That leaves the church with no choice but to build its behavioral models assuming that believers should strive for a more complete, committed fellowship of love. Models based on individual autonomy are simply inadequate from a Christian point of view.

Dealing with Disparities

The second advantage of the model deals with the large disparities in life style that exist among Christians of the same church. Where these disparities exist through circumstance and not choice, very little effective interaction can occur. One economist, in discussing the need to have communities of faith disciple each other on matters of consumption, writes, "We will not be successful in becoming an effective 'consumption watchers' group for each other unless we deal with the differences in income levels among us. I cannot help you to deal with your desires if my income is higher than yours and if I insist it is my income alone, to spend as I choose."[2] It is clear in the context in which it is written that this reference to income corresponds to the consumption part of the model developed here.

To see more clearly why consumption differences create barriers to communication, visualize a hypothetical lawyer who spends sixty thousand dollars a year on his family, telling a hypothetical elementary school teacher, who spends nineteen thousand dollars a year on his family, not to eat out in a restaurant, to forego a vacation, to get a baby sitter and have his wife work, or to abandon family plans for a third child. Since the lawyer has made no similar adjustments, the interchange that follows could sound like this:

Teacher: It doesn't seem fair that I must make these adjustments when you can live as you please.
Lawyer: Why not? I earn my income, so there is no reason why I can't spend it.
Teacher: But I work as long and as hard as you do and my job helps society as much as yours.
Lawyer: If that were true, your pay would equal mine.

From here the discussion degenerates quickly.

Teacher: Not so. Your pay is higher because the legal profession has created a monopoly for itself in order to charge unrealistically high

---

2. Henry Rempel, "Our Role in the World Food Crisis," *Church, Industry and Business Association* (July 1976): 5.

rates. The law profession even resisted the law allowing their members to advertise charges.

Lawyer: Not so. Nothing stopped you from entering law school and competing with me.

Teacher: . . . .

These discussions rarely, if ever, occur among church members because of the dissensions and hard feelings that would result. But how many times have exchanges similar to this one occurred in people's minds, and what has been the effect of these thoughts on the life of the fellowship? To prevent these thoughts, church people have hidden their financial affairs from view as much as possible. The lawyer wants to be appreciated, so he will try not to flaunt his income; the teacher wants respect, so he will hide his financial struggles. Both need each other in the church. One has teaching skills, the other can help meet the budget and give counsel to the church, but the atmosphere of love and sharing and trust does not exist.[3]

Some suggest that low-income persons truly committed to Christ will not be affected by income disparities in the church, so that this conversation is unrealistic. This is true if the church has implicitly or explicitly defined an appropriate consumption range that includes both the teacher and the lawyer. However, if no such range is defined, each individual will define for himself what a Christian life style should be. The confusion that results detracts from congregational unity, hindering the mission of the church. The least it must do is to help the person in need, but if there is no understanding of the definition of need, how can it do this?

A wealthy person buys an air conditioner, a dishwasher, a set of golf clubs, or a van to meet a "need." Yet a poor person who comes to the church for help expressing those same needs probably will not be accommodated. The church is forced into the position of saying that the rich and the poor, in many areas of life, do not have the same needs, or that the rich should be allowed to consume

---

3. The barriers created between people by disparate consumption and income levels are illustrated well in an article by Jon Bonk, "The Role of Affluence in the Christian Missionary Enterprise from the West," *Missiology: An International Review,* vol. 14, no. 4 (October 1986). Although this article is concerned mainly with foreign mission situations, the message is relevant within cultures as well as between cultures.

above their needs in areas of luxury. Hiding this dilemma with the hope that strong commitment on the part of the poor will make the problem disappear means exposing oneself to severe temptation.

What are people really saying when they declare publicly or by action that they have the right to live at a standard much above that of the other members in the church? They are suggesting, first, that they deserve more because of their skills, ability, or value to society, and second, that they were fortunate enough to be at the right place at the right time. In other words, they were smart, hard working, lucky, or all three. Yet a good mind and good fortune are gifts from God to his church, not to individuals, and a person's contribution to production is a response to God for those gifts. How many times have we heard individuals testify how the Lord has blessed them? Yet from 1 Corinthians 12 it is clear that the blessing was meant for the church to share and profit from in love: "There are different kinds of gifts, but the same Spirit. There are different kinds of service, but the same Lord. There are different kinds of working, but the same God works all of them in all men. Now to each one the manifestation of the Spirit is given for the common good" (vv. 4–7).

Later in this passage Paul indicates that those with less glamorous skills are blessed no less by God, even though their monetary income may not be great. To be intelligent and lucky, from God's point of view, entitles one to no more or less consumption because of those blessings, even if it does bring a person high income. High earnings come to those with productive gifts, and they should not reduce their work effort simply because their consumption may not rise with their income.

If these views are present in the church, believers will desire to find ways to close the large life style gaps in the church. The model presented here can help in this effort.

The Blessing of the Church

The third advantage of this model is that, if they apply it, believers will have the blessing of the church on their life style. This will minimize the suspicions and mistrust that can occur otherwise, as well as the guilt that some feel because of uncertainty regarding their standard of living. It will never remove the tension of consuming in a world of scarcity, but the tension is shared by the community of faith and provides a constant reminder to that community that all life-style norms need review from time to time. Such a review will insure that the fourth advantage of the model is achieved: that all resource use, not just 10 percent, will be considered as part of the witness of faith and subject to the blessing of the community of faith.

Being Salt and Light

The fifth advantage, providing a witness to the larger society, fits into the church's function as salt and light to the world (Matt. 5:13–14). It is not necessary to document the despair of many in the secular kingdom, both rich and poor, who have made the struggle for increased living standards a religion as they serve *mammon* as their god. This is one way the church can show that it has a better, more meaningful way of meeting the material needs of people.

Current attempts at mutual sharing through church-sponsored insurance programs have successfully re-integrated into the church some functions that the church earlier abandoned. For example, the Mennonite denomination has its own investment fund, a congregational college tuition-sharing program, auto and health insurance programs, retirement centers, disaster service organizations, and many local sharing services.

Years ago I was a member of a denominational regional auto insurance plan. There had been a rather heavy claim one year, so the pool of funds for claims had fallen below the desirable level. Instead of raising the premiums, the company sent a letter to all members explaining the problem and asking for donations according to the members' ability to pay. The donations eliminated the problem. Another feature of that insurance arrangement was that every six months a list of names with claims paid was sent to all members. There was some incentive to avoid claims since no one wanted to be an obvious drain on the fund.

Many denominations have similar programs and others are forming. There is no reason why this experience shouldn't encourage the church to support more localized efforts that may illustrate to society that Christianity does make a difference at the

financial level. The church at large should be building evidence
that Christianity has a significant economic impact on the lives of
those who profess it.

Giving Guidance

The sixth advantage of the model relates to the direction that
the model, functioning effectively, gives to those who are asking
serious questions about their financial involvement in secular
society. For example, relevant questions might be:

1. Should I invest money in the stock of a company that produces weapons or tobacco or even luxury items that have
   little, if any, functional use?
2. In what companies is the endowment of the college I support
   invested?
3. Are the business practices of the companies I invest in just
   and fair to the consumer, and does that matter?
4. Should I work where I must join and support a militant
   union that demands pay hikes far above productivity
   growth?
5. As an employee, what responsibility do I have in a firm
   whose business ethics are unchristian (e.g., discrimination
   or payoffs)?

All of these questions and more are difficult to answer with an
across-the-board response. Each is a special case and demands the
attention of a fellowship that can approach the situation with less
bias than can any one person. When the majority feeling of the
group grows into consensus, the decision is made and the binding
and loosing process can occur. This process cannot be taken
lightly. For example, in Wisconsin, seven Catholic religious communities have formed an organization to research investment
sources, looking for those that benefit society from the Christian
point of view. At least one mutual fund investment company
serves those who seek investments in industries where no war-
related products are produced, fair employment practices are followed, and international development is fostered.[4] Many other

---

4. Leon Lukaszewski, "Let's Get Moral About Money," *U.S. Catholic,* vol. 40
(February 1975): 13.

funds have special moral criteria for investing as well, and new ones could be formed. When believers get serious about moral dimensions of economic behavior, many creative expressions of faith can develop.

Gaining Strength from the Group

The last listed advantage of the model, that of deeper involvement in the fellowship, involves a principle of human nature well known to the Christian and the non-Christian. When difficult tasks lie ahead, group support and specific measures of progress are invaluable in bringing results.

For example, most people recognize that physical exercise is necessary for good health. Yet it is a rare individual who continues an exercise program faithfully alone. Successful joggers jog with others. The discipline of the friend helps to overcome the monotony and drudgery of the task. Also, specific measures reveal when the goal is reached. Jogging became more meaningful to many when they realized that two miles run in under fifteen minutes three times a week could provide enough exercise for good health. Without a defined goal and a support group, difficult tasks become impossible. The same is true in Weight Watchers, Alcoholics Anonymous, prepared childbirth, or any other task that requires hard work and discipline. The Christian life requires the same dedication and discipline.

One of the tasks that requires hard work and discipline is responsible resource use. How unfortunate that few Christians work hard to establish life-style norms and support each other in living consistently with them! It is meaningful and enjoyable to find ways to conserve; having less must become more satisfying than having more. By developing a spirit of unity in action, Christians can grow into a deeper involvement in faith with each other.

Objections to the Model

Before leaving the discussion of the formal model, we need to look at some of the criticisms or concerns that many have about its operation.

1. High-income earners may have less incentive to earn income if it is not for themselves, and so their productivity may drop.
2. Some may prefer to receive a church grant rather than to work.
3. The group decision process involves people in decisions in areas where they have no expertise or training.
4. How can one insure that the group is not simply a collection of friends that gives its blessing to any whimsical request? In other words, what keeps the group balanced?

All of these questions are legitimate and must be taken seriously. The first and second concerns have similar answers: they involve people whose commitment to the fellowship and its purpose is weak. Christians who amass wealth to live in luxury rather than for the service they can perform with it are out of step with the spirit of Scripture and would benefit from a careful study of biblical teaching. If their wealth is not viewed as a tool for service to God and the church, it is unlikely that they will be attracted to a community of faith in the first place—particularly if the teaching of the church is clear and the discipling task of believers is being practiced. Furthermore, a believer is productive in response to God's sufficiency and grace. If less is retained personally and more is given away, the incentive for the Christian to work should not diminish. In fact, when a life of giving is practiced, the joy that results is usually incentive to do more rather than less.

The rich young man of Matthew 19:16–22 wanted to become part of the kingdom of God, but when he realized that his wealth had to be brought under submission, he rejected the kingdom voluntarily. It is interesting that Christ was not inclined to back away from his high demands in order to keep from alienating the rich man, who was probably a faithful tither. Likewise the church should be clear on its expectations in the area of resource use.

The situation may differ for the person who sees the church as an escape from work. There are those who will apply for consumption grants continuously, seeking a free ride while they contribute little. To counter this, each grant request must be accompanied by full supporting data documenting the reason for the need. Some in the church may be commissioned to involve themselves in worthwhile tasks that do not pay wages or, at best, pay inadequate wages. These would receive grants in the same way missionaries and volunteer workers presently do. In those cases Christians are not offended by those who attempt to raise their own support for service activity.

In other cases, emergencies may arise requiring financial help to fill the gap between needs and income. In still other cases, there may be those who legitimately cannot find work or have handicaps that restrict earnings below the acceptable level. In all cases, no one should receive grants without careful review.

The discipling process in these matters involves balancing several principles taught in Scripture. On the one side is the admonition to "bear your own burden" and not be lazy (Gal. 6:5; 2 Thess. 3:10; Rom. 12:11). On the other side is the command to help a brother or sister in need and to bear one another's burdens (Gal. 6:2; Rom. 12:13; 1 John 3:17). There is no indication that these could not include financial burdens, even though the context of some of the passages refers to moral faults. Decisions on consumption grants will not be easy, especially when admonition is required, but if taken seriously the process can reward everyone involved.

Nevertheless, the model we are examining should make the process work better because it defines need by the lower level of the consumption range instead of not defining it at all. At present, the church has the same directives regarding the poor that this model suggests, but it has a very unstructured way of approaching the problem. Thus it never articulates clearly who really needs help and who needs appropriate encouragement to be productive.

The third objection to the model concerns the decision process. The dynamics of any group are such that those with expertise in a particular area are looked to for leadership in that area. Certainly those within a group who know little about business will not have a strong influence on whether the fellowship affirms a business person's plans for investment. The important point is that the person in business must describe his intentions, goals, and proposals so that less knowledgeable people can give their support on the grounds of what they can understand and of their trust in the person involved. This process will help the businessman to keep before him in his planning the kingdom goals to which he has committed himself as a member of the church.

One other concern about the decision process is the *decision rule* that is followed. Perhaps the best statement of the decision rule is one of majority rule in the framework of consensus. Those who have a political orientation toward decision making and have never shared in a fellowship based on Christian love will have a difficult time interpreting a process so ambiguous. Where agreement by acclamation isn't possible, the issue is debated, researched, and prayed about. Votes are taken and the will of the majority is then supported by all those in the fellowship in a manner similar to the current process of choosing congregational officers. The greater the sharing of Christian love in the fellowship, the greater will be the appropriation of the Holy Spirit and the more satisfactory the discerning process.

The last criticism deals with the moorings of the group itself. What keeps it from serving its own interests rather than the purposes of God?

True, some fellowships have departed from a serious effort to become the people of God. They reinforce each other's biases and accomplish little. However, it is far easier for individuals to deviate from a commitment on their own than for groups to deviate from the same commitment. What keeps Weight Watchers from encouraging obesity, or Alcoholics Anonymous from throwing huge drinking parties? The answer lies in each group's avowed purpose and commitment to a goal. Alone, it is easy to falter in commitment. The group acts as a balance wheel, constantly calling back into the fold those who are tempted to stray.

The community of believers is that balance wheel for the Christian. If the group is serious about its faith and uses Scripture as its anchor, it has a far better chance of serving the kingdom of God effectively than do individuals apart from a group. When a fellowship loses its moorings and no persuasive voice within it calls for renewal, the kingdom of God ceases to be served in that gathering, but this is unlikely to occur until long after the individuals, on their own, have departed from the faith.

Discussion Questions

1. In what sense is the model developed here radical?
2. For many, this chapter goes from preaching to meddling. Do you agree or disagree with this statement? How can you tell the difference?

3. The issues of productive and nonproductive investment have been debated in some form or another for many years. Some argue that any use of money is ultimately productive and the distinction is useless. Would you put different values on the acquisition of gold or nonsentimental antiques than you would on a farm implement if each of these expenditures brought the same return on your money? If so, why? If not, why not?

4. Was your standard of living arrived at by a careful and prayerful consideration of what is right or has it evolved through a justification process of arguing that it is not wrong?

5. Do churches today have enough of the 1 Corinthians 12 and 13 qualities to practice the model suggested here? If so, give examples as exhibits to encourage others to follow. If not, what can be done to change the situation?

6. If you are perturbed by this chapter, analyze what parts of it were offensive and why you feel as you do.

7. If you are sympathetic with the message of this chapter, analyze why you feel as you do.

8. What are the implications of questions 6 and 7 if feelings divide along income or consumption lines?

9. In your opinion, is the basic unit of Christian action the church or the individual? Support your view with appropriate biblical material.

7

The Model Illustrated

Many excellent examples of Christian community scattered across the country could provide good case studies of the model at work. I have chosen three real ones and one hypothetical one to represent a varied selection of the qualities that make a community of faith work.

The first story is of my own personal pilgrimage. Through experience I have become convinced that the kingdom of God can break through in economic matters and become the reference point for all economic behavior. I do not live in a commune or similar intentional community. I have one car and a comfortable home in a suburb of a major city. I have two children and a below-average income for the community, but above-average income when compared with national standards. I offer my story partly to illustrate that I am a fellow pilgrim in the search for responsible stewardship, not one who can speak from glowing success. My conviction on these matters has kept me stewardship conscious, but in the world of specifics, I find the applications difficult.

Perhaps my earliest recollection of the involvement of the community of faith in the life of its people came when a farm accident disabled my father for a year. Many people in the church were also farmers, and tractors and equipment descended on our fields so that in two days the entire corn crop was in storage. That was followed by a blank check for labor from the Christian brothers for any farm duties we could not handle ourselves. Our brothers and sisters in the church responded spontaneously to the financial emergencies that followed, and, although it was a difficult year for us, I remember feeling that the church stood firmly between us and extreme financial uncertainty and despair. I learned through this experience that a community rather than a self-sufficiency orientation brings out the best in a church.

It is not completely clear to me yet how significant these early experiences were in my later thinking, but this and similar examples of the Mennonite tradition of collective caring and sharing have made an indelible impression that will influence what I believe, teach, and do for the rest of my life.

Throughout high school and college I had the advantage of not being rich, so it was easy for me to live in a manner consistent with my emerging feeling that the Christian calling involved a commitment to a more controlled life style than the American dream entailed. On graduating from college, I bought the simplest economical new car on the market and took a job as a social worker in a medium-sized city.

Fortunately, there was a small, cohesive Mennonite fellowship there for me to relate to. The caring and sharing that had been collective now became much more personal. I felt myself responding to the fellowship not out of duty but out of love for my brothers and sisters. I adopted the norms that evolved within the church because of my desire to identify with the group and because I had, along with everyone else, a role in establishing the norms. It became clear to me that the legalism that accompanies large-scale collective caring can be replaced by an environment of personal caring and love from which group norms evolve. These norms are willingly aspired to by the community of believers because they want to be identified as members of the fellowship.

Two years later, when I left that community, I took a vision of what a community of faith could become, although the economic issues of life style and business practice had not been key concerns on which group norms had evolved. This was true perhaps because most of the members were young and did not earn incomes that allowed a resource-intensive life style. I also married during my last year as a social worker, and life-style decisions became family decisions. My wife shared my basic stewardship ideas, but being on the same wavelength is not the same as agreeing on all the details.

It is not surprising to me now that my occupational interests evolved from social studies to social work to economics. Somehow the cutting edge of every issue seemed to center on matters in the economic area of life. However, few voices within Christianity were speaking on economic issues. Most believers seemed all too ready to accept society's solutions to economic questions.

My graduate experience was significant not only because of what I learned in economics but also because of the association my wife and I had with a community of believers. That fellowship taught us much about what it means to live in God's kingdom. Again this church happened to be a fellowship in which the community tradition was historically rooted. From this base the functions of the church were carried out in numerous ways. The festival of faith and worship occurred each Sunday with a wide range of participation. The intimacy of *koinonia* came through weekly meetings of a smaller subset of the congregation that entered into specific, mutual commitments to apply faith better. Regularly scheduled congregational business meetings provided a forum for collective administration in the church. Although the church had its share of weaknesses and shortcomings, it attempted to apply biblical teaching to all areas of life, including economic issues of life style. In a general way it discouraged extravagance, but what was more important was the informal process by which extravagance was defined. Members who sought guidance on major purchases received the best input that those in the fellowship could give.

I remember very well bringing our household budget to a meeting where this information was shared by each one in hopes of providing support and guidance for future spending. I recall feeling the need to make some adjustments in our family spending pattern. Decisions arrived at in this manner are easier to carry out if friends can be depended on to encourage and challenge each other to meet their goals. The significant point of this experience is that economic decisions on life style had become integrated into my expression of faith, and the fellowship of believers had accepted some degree of discerning and discipling function in this important area.

When I finished graduate studies and we had to make a choice regarding employment, the fellowship confirmed our feeling that we could serve God's kingdom better in the lower-paying of two alternative jobs, even though the higher-paying offer was tempting.

Two months after leaving that fellowship, my wife's youngest brother died in an automobile accident. On our way to the funeral we spent an evening with the believers of that fellowship. They had gathered to share our grief, and their hurt was not superficial. We left for the funeral reassured that significant Christian love had been a part of our experience with that community of believers. Without that love, issues—particularly economic ones—become divisive and irritating.

Today the issues are less clear than they were in graduate school. We own a modest home by the standards of our town, but the county we live in is one of the more wealthy in the country. Furthermore, a good portion of the student body and the constituency of the school where I work are inclined to see a high-consumption life style as God's blessing to them rather than as a dangerous obstacle to their faith and witness.

A congregation that believes in the dangers of materialism, a renewed joy in giving that comes from work on stewardship goals at the denomination level, a small group that attempts to practice the model I have described, and occasional involvement in inner-city churches in Chicago have convinced me that a believer must continue to swim upstream against the materialistic current of our time. It is not easy but it can be a joy, not a burden. The process is slow and uncertain, but somewhere behind it all is an awareness that life style and business practice are important areas of concern for the church in twentieth-century America. No Christian can take decisions involving the world's scarce resources lightly.

This long personal story serves only to illustrate in a non-theoretical framework why I believe God's kingdom can break through meaningfully in difficult areas of life. I also hope it will make the model presented in the previous chapter seem more plausible. But it cannot provide answers to other people's situations. In many ways the answers are not as important as the process because the questions change from year to year.

Economic Decision Making in Fellowship Groups

The next case is a hypothetical one using a congregation named Alpha and a small fellowship group within it named Beta. Alpha is a large, established congregation of four hundred members, most of whom attend regularly. It performs the functions of corporate celebration of faith, group education, and worship each Sunday morning. It provides a social base for fellowship and has a strong collective help program in the community and the world beyond. Alpha has a paid minister and a committee structure that facilitates the fulfillment of these functions. It provides a superstructure for the individual Christian to identify with and relate to on many issues. But it teaches principles and general applications; in many ways it is impersonal because of its size. Members know each other's names and may visit each other's homes occasionally, but it is not an intimate group in a personal sense.

Within Alpha is a subset of Christians who voluntarily gathered to work out some of the more specific applications of faith. Beta formed not because members were disillusioned with Alpha but because they realized that Alpha could not possibly serve all of the biblical functions of the New Testament church. Beta consists of six families representing a cross-section of the congregation. Before joining together they had had mutual respect for each other, developed from casual observation of each other's participation in the church, so the members were not randomly selected. They have in common a strong desire to grow spiritually and a belief that growth can best be achieved in the context of an intimate, caring group. They have committed themselves to each other as fellow disciples in the faith and have pledged to give a specific block of time each week for meeting. They also have covenanted together to share Christian love, support, and discipline in an attempt to work out more faithfully the teachings of Jesus in their social, economic, political, and physical environment.

Beta does not compete with Alpha. On doctrinal issues and the sacramental functions of the church, Alpha is the center for activity. If Beta has problems it cannot handle itself, Alpha is the first resource it taps. Alpha is supported fully by all members of Beta, and Beta is seen as the instrument that can help carry out the full functions of the church.

The concern here is to explore Beta's activity in the economic area in hopes of seeing how some aspects of the model can be practiced. Life style was one of the last things Beta tackled; thus, when someone posed questions in this area, the members expressed themselves freely.

The issue arose when one couple (Jack and Alice Delta) made plans to purchase a new house. They asked for help in deciding the size and quality of house to build. The word from the Lord was extremely unclear to them. Jack said that he had eighty thousand dollars of equity in his old house that he would use for downpayment. His salary could easily allow payments on a mortgage of one hundred thousand dollars. The average home in the area where they lived was ninety thousand dollars, but the new house they were considering was in an exclusive neighborhood where $180,000 was about average.

At first the group was excited about the possibility of the Deltas' new home, but then Jack asked what the group thought Jesus might advise if he were there. Here is the conversation that followed:

Jack: Last night I read in Matthew about the dangers of laying up treasures on earth. Would I be doing that?

Sam: Well, it is true that a house is essentially a consumption item in many ways.

Jack: At work they tell me it is a good investment, in other words, a sound financial move as well as good housing.

Sam: Nearly all realized appreciation on homes is put back into more expensive homes. This appreciation, which is the investment side of the purchase, never gets into productive investment where society at large benefits. It usually ends up encouraging even more consumption by placing people in bigger houses. Take the appreciation on your present home. Where is it going? Into better housing for you. But don't knock yourself, the tax laws almost force people to do this. Look at how God has blessed you! He has given you open doors. What are you waiting for?

Jack: All I need is the blessing of the community of faith. That's where you people come in. If Jesus is here, it is by his spirit, who is imparted best in the context of this fellowship.

Joan: I haven't the faintest idea what to tell you, Jack. We will never have a decision like that to make ourselves because we can barely meet our rent each month, let alone save for a down payment. All I do is look at *Better Homes and Gardens* and dream what I'll do when I win a sweepstakes.

Diane: If there weren't so much poverty downtown and around the world, I'd feel much better about the whole idea.

Alex: Let's approach it this way: How much space and convenience do you need?

Jack: We would like a spare bedroom, and I need a study at home. Alice would like a rough play area for the kids so the family room isn't such a mess when guests come. Our house now has only room air conditioners that cool only part of the house, so central air would be a big help. Then there's the yard, which would sure beat the public park as a play area. Beyond that we need very little.

Alex: Do most of the rest of you feel these are needs a Christian should fulfill?

Joan: I would like all those things too, but the fact that I get along pretty well without them now makes me wonder if they are really needs. What do you think, Helen? Life hasn't been easy for you lately.

Helen: I don't know, Joan. Since Pete died and I had to begin a job, I've not been sure whether loneliness or lack of money is my bigger problem. I know that without some of you chipping in I would never have made it. Anyway, at this point the kind of life style Jack is talking about is so far from my thinking that I really can't give any advice offhand.

Sam: In my background life-style questions were individual matters. Has that changed?

Jack: That was my experience too, Sam, but one reason why we got together as a committed group of believers was that we felt some of the existing patterns were not meeting our needs for spiritual growth. In my experience, the economic issues of life are my biggest spiritual blind spot.

Sam: You're right, Jack, but we obviously need more time and study to be of much help.

At this point the group resolved to prepare for careful Bible study on life-style matters and Jack decided to hold off on his house building. The weekly meetings that followed were difficult. Some couldn't feel right about Jack's proposed house as long as Helen was unable to have more than basic food and housing. Helen insisted that God would provide in his own time or had a reason for her unfortunate circumstances, and that Jack's decision was not related to her situation. Most did not agree with Helen, saying that the body-of-Christ model implied that if Helen suffered, Jack suffered, too.

Finally, around New Year's, the group decided to bring together their financial records of the past year. Their earning and spending patterns, as well as their giving and investing, were included. It was a long but fruitful evening. Everyone set consumption and charity goals for the new year. The group decided to take one meeting in June to check on the progress of the budgeting. They prayed that God would help them not to consume more than they ought and that he would provide in those cases where necessary consumption exceeded anticipated income, as was the case with Helen and a few others.

What happened? Did Jack build his big house? How many did not meet their goals? Did God provide for Helen, and if so, how? Those questions are for you to answer. All that can be said is that the process was carried through each year and, strangely enough, the range of consumption levels within the group became narrower, even though the income range did not. The members became more aware of resource use and its implications on life style. The community of faith became a much more cohesive launching pad for its members.

Other groups formed within Alpha and the congregation became a more dynamic testimony to the power of God in people's lives. However, all is not perfect in Alpha. Some say that too many restrictions are put on the life style of some members because of the implicit expectations of the church. People have even left the church because of this. Others feel that the church is not disciplining enough because annual consumption goals are determined by individuals themselves, even if they do consult the counsel of their fellowship groups.

More recently, several business people in the church have shared some business financial information with their small group. The group had little to offer at first, but eagerly learned about some of the business issues that are concerns of believing business people. The process itself helped the business people maintain an awareness of the claims of Christ on their businesses, and it also helped the non-business people in the group gain a new appreciation for the way believers may influence others in their business dealings.

The exciting part was that the claims of the gospel were brought specifically to bear on economic decisions, alongside all the secular claims that bombard individuals. In other words, Jesus finally had a strong lobby working for him in the minds of his people, and it was making a difference.

Financial Counsel in Small Groups

The next two examples are true. They illustrate how some of the qualities of a community of faith can be applied in a very simple setting without formal institutional trappings. Each case is told by a person involved in the story.

Case 1

For several years I have been part of a small fellowship that meets for breakfast once each week. We have met primarily for fellowship and mutual encouragement in the faith. The group consists of men with various educational backgrounds and vocations. Because we have relied on each other for feedback in the tough areas of faith, the fellowship has been a useful resource for establishing better accountability in our Christian life.

Personal finance has been a topic of frequent discussion. I recall one period when we were discussing the role of debt in managing our family budgets. Several in the group had been reading and thinking in this area and trying to relate the issue to biblical principles. Over several weeks we began, as individuals, to question the role of debt and its burden on the monthly budget. It seemed to us that a budget that has little flexibility because of debt restricts freedom to give and leads to a spiritually unhealthy preoccupation with material concerns. We especially questioned the use of debt to finance luxury items that depreciate in value.

The group is informal and we make no attempt to force majority opinion on anyone. But in one instance, one of the men reevaluated his family's purchase of a fairly expensive travel van on credit. He felt that the burden of the monthly payments put an unnecessary strain on his budget. He also felt that the consumption of this luxury good had become a lesser value. He decided to sell the van, pay off the debt, and use the remainder of the proceeds to purchase a lower-cost vehicle for cash.

Now, after two years, he looks back on the experience with a great deal of satisfaction and has on numerous occasions expressed his appreciation for the way in which our small breakfast fellowship has influenced his Christian life, even in resource use. I believe each of us could relate personal instances where our financial and vocational decisions have been shaped or altered because of the insights gained from this group.

Case 2

The members of our church fellowship believe that Scripture says much about responsible stewardship. One example of how this belief was lived out occurred one year when a member wanted to buy a home for his family. While looking, the family realized that the obligation of a mortgage and the preoccupation of home ownership could detract from what they viewed as their real mission. Because of this they sought the counsel of fellow believers to help in the decision.

When they found a house that seemed to fill their needs, they came to me and asked me to help them figure out whether the financial obligation of the house would fit their budget. "We will trust your judgment," they told me, "because you have more experience and expertise in these matters than we do."

I went over their income data and balance sheet and was concerned that the family was not in a position financially to purchase the house. Yet I knew they had invested so much time searching that backing out would be a disappointment. It was hard for me finally to tell them that I felt it was not wise to buy the house just then. I suggested that they try to save the difference between their rent and the mortgage payments they would have made on the house for at least a year. If they could do that, they would have both a better down payment and the confidence that they could meet the payments.

One year later the ideal house opened up a stone's throw from where they were renting, and they had the money to make the purchase. The house has served them well over the years and the experience has confirmed in at least their minds and mine that God was at work in the economic areas of life. One by-product of the experience was that our trust and respect for each other deepened.

The Communal Option

The last case involves a different institutional structure from the previous examples. So far in this book there has been no mention of communes, in which a common treasury is used and discipling sometimes takes on an authoritarian tone. This has been deliberate for several reasons. First, most believers find those forms of religious and social organization so far removed from their experience that they appear irrelevant. Second, the Christian commune movement, which flourished in the 1960s and early 1970s, has gone through a period of re-evaluation and adjustment that has led to a substantial reduction in the numbers of believers who share common treasury experiences.

Perhaps the most stimulating case study of a communal experience is the book *Glimpses of Glory*, which describes the thirty-year journey of Reba Place Fellowship in Evanston, Illinois.[1] This book is a candid look at the substantial benefits and costs of intense community life. From this experience at least four prerequisites for a successful common-treasury, intentional community experience stand out. First, each person involved must have a strong commitment to the group and to the idea that God can make it work. Second, each must be willing to accept the discipline of the elders or leaders when uniform decisions are required. Third, a belief that service to God and others can be maximized more through a centralized community than through a decentralized congregational approach is important if communal living is to succeed. Fourth, the community family rather than the nuclear family unit must become the place where the pretenses of life are stripped away and security in social relationships develops.

Reba Place Fellowship began in 1957 with "a vision for 'being the church' in the city, a disciplined brotherhood which took discipleship seriously, including a common treasury and corporate decision making as a means of giving up self and seeking the will of

---

1. Dave Jackson and Neta Jackson, *Glimpses of Glory: Thirty Years of Community* (Elgin, Ill.: Brethren, 1987). This study is one of several that gives helpful insights into the dynamics of communal living. Another, describing the Woodcrest bruderhof community in New York, is by Ulrich Eggers, *Community for Life* (Scottdale, Penn.: Herald, 1980). A historical treatment of communal living is Trevor J. Saxby's *Pilgrims of a Common Life* (Scottdale, Penn.: Herald, 1987).

God together. . . . The fellowship houses—as many as 15—were converted into extended family households of 12–24 persons, settings for support, life-style ministry and intensive counseling."[2]

By 1987 the Fellowship had evolved into a combination of households and cluster groups that were less focused on internal ministry and inner healing and more involved in mission outreach and service. Most members are not involved in the common treasury, but the concern for responsible stewardship is still important to members whether they are in the common treasury or manage their own family budgets.

The story of the thirty years of Reba Place history, as presented in *Glimpses of Glory,* is one of triumph and discouragement. God's grace and human frailty were brought together by a deep commitment that changed many lives. For Reba Place Fellowship, the economic component of community life is described in one section of a Vision Paper dated May 20, 1980, and called kingdom economics:

renouncing all to follow Christ
trusting that God will provide our economic needs, first through
    the Christian community
seeking first the Kingdom
working hard, praying, being good stewards of money and material resources
avoiding accumulation, traveling light, living simply
being content, avoiding covetousness
investing in the Kingdom, giving generously, sharing income and
    assets as much as possible, especially giving to the poor
daily bread—minimizing storing up for the future and borrowing
    against the future.[3]

There is evidence that these ideals were practiced in the fertile soil of the intense communal experience of Reba Place Fellowship. There is also reason to believe that these values can continue to guide the congregational members of Reba Place today who are not in the common treasury.

It has been a thesis of this book that Christians everywhere

2. Jackson and Jackson, *Glimpses,* p. 16.
3. Ibid., p. 314.

should strive to clarify the kingdom economics that should be lived out in their lives and that community life in some form is essential to the clarification and living process. Most will not make dramatic plunges into communal forms of economic decision making, but the blessing that will result from adjustments on the edges of our economic decisions might well open new doors of witness and service. After all, it was only curiosity that started Zacchaeus on his way to an enormous change in his economic way of life (Luke 19:1–10).

Discussion Questions

1. Can you sketch the experiences that formed your view of the church? How important are other believers in the decision process when you make important choices?
2. If you were Jack, what would you do after the discussion described in this chapter?
3. Which of the following alternatives describes your feeling about this chapter?
   a. The model is just not realistic for our society and does not fit my understanding of what Christians should do.
   b. This model is an appropriate ideal model for Christians to work toward, but it is not likely to work in real life.
   c. This model is an appropriate ideal model that Christians should apply in whatever ways they can.
4. Create your own list of kingdom economic values and contrast them with the Reba Place list.
5. Some people thrive in a communal experience while others find it oppressive. What accounts for the differences and how should they be addressed by a community of faith?

8

Individual Freedom and Private Property:
The First Pillar

The next four chapters discuss a few key, underlying ideas of the secular economic system of markets without offering a qualifying critique from a Christian vantage point. The critique will come in a later chapter. For now it is important to examine capitalism on its own terms. In some ways these chapters caricature the tenets of market capitalism, because it is impossible to explore a complicated economic system in depth in a few brief chapters.

The bare essentials of a market economic system were touched on in chapters 1 and 2. The price system as an allocator, with its tie-in to production, has been discussed already. However, the mechanics of any system are meaningless apart from the ideas that undergird its operation. The ideology of market capitalism is closely tied to its practice and has important policy implications. How we think about the way the world works conditions our approach to policy. In other words, to relate effectively to markets one must understand how they work and what ideology drives them. In this endeavor we venture beyond market mechanics and into the larger topic of market capitalism, which encompasses the social, philosophical, and historical dimensions of societal organization.

Building on the concept developed earlier of a price system of allocation, at least three components of a market environment form the social system often called capitalism. First is the concept of individual freedom, symbolized best in the institution of private property. Second is the view that social and economic harmony result if people, operating within defined rules of the game, pursue their own best interests, a concept considered in chapter 9. Third is belief in carefully defined limits on governmental intervention in the economy, an idea discussed in chapter 10. Each of these issues will be discussed at some length to illustrate the difficulty of simplistic conclusions about the positives and negatives of market capitalism.

Individual Freedom and Social Organization

Friedrich A. Hayek, a leading social theorist of this century, has done much to defend the view that individual freedom is essential to social organization.[1] Hayek, in contrast to less astute social thinkers, who argue for freedom merely because it feels better than bondage, builds his understanding of natural liberty on the belief that social institutions and cultural characteristics are far too complex and historically rooted to be altered successfully by central planning. The belief that people created social institutions and therefore can alter them in socially beneficial ways is, in Hayek's view, incorrect.

If no blueprint went into the development of a social institution like language, for example, then no blueprint will effectively change that institution. The only goal of policy makers should be to structure rules that will prevent antisocial behavior, by which Hayek means behavior that hurts or coerces others.

---

1. Among the major works of Hayek are *The Constitution of Liberty: Law, Legislation and Liberty* (Chicago: University of Chicago Press, 1960) and *Road to Serfdom* (Chicago: University of Chicago Press, 1944). A small but informative summary of Hayek's ideas can be found in the book by Eamonn Butler, *Hayek* (New York: University Books, 1983). The examples listed in the following paragraphs are found in various sources from Hayek, including *Studies in Philosophy, Politics, and Economics* (Chicago: University of Chicago Press, Midway Reprint Series, 1980), pp. 69–70 (bees) and *The Counter-Revolution of Science: Studies on the Abuse of Reason* (London and New York: The Free Press of Glencoe/Collier-Macmillan, 1955), chap. 4 (footpaths).

Some of Hayek's examples are helpful in understanding this idea. In addition to language, which simply grew spontaneously over time without a designer, beehives and footpaths are examples of how society develops. Bees have orderly functions and a hive can be a complex society, yet no hive is planned by a bright, intellectual bee. Footpaths develop as people walk from place to place because people independently find the same best route between two points and benefit by chance from each other's actions as the path hardens. Many a sidewalk builder has been frustrated when trying to plan where people should walk rather than building where they do. To carry this analogy further, society is better off if it engages only in rule making that puts necessary limits on behavior that hurts others. Prohibiting walkers from trampling someone's garden is appropriate, but designing the path is excessive social planning.

This spontaneous evolutionary development of the social order leads to the most desirable outcomes in economic life as well. Economic relationships are like footpaths. They evolve over time so that exchange arrangements, which we call markets, develop. Intervening in markets is like trying to build sidewalks where an architect, without regard to walkers' preferences, would prefer them to be. The market intervention will be no more successful and probably as wasteful as the unused concrete sidewalks. The best economic policy protects property rights of market participants in the same way that the best sidewalk policy creates a rule against walking in gardens. Maximum freedom is retained, and optimal social organization can continue to evolve.

The manner in which markets contribute to desirable social organization should be explored further. When people are free to follow their interests and have exchangeable rights of ownership, opportunities for improvement become apparent. As long as people value items differently, there is a chance for both parties to gain from an exchange.

For example, suppose I win a car and you win a two-week cruise, but each of us would prefer the other's prize. If we exchanged prizes, both of us would be better off. If we never knew each other and made the exchange voluntarily through a middleman who made some profit on the deal, then all three parties would be better off. As long as each transaction is voluntary and ownership rights are clear, the gains are realized.

However, if the whole world had keys to the car and I had no
title, the car would be nearly worthless to me in both use and
exchange, since everyone would want it, even for trivial uses, it
being free for the taking. The tragedy of this breakdown in property rights is that the car would only rarely be used for its most
socially valuable purpose, since a doctor on an emergency call
would have no more claim on it than would teenagers on a joy
ride. Somehow, ownership must be assigned to someone who can
prevent free use of the car.

But even if ownership is assigned to the teenagers, the doctor
will use the car. Why? Because it is worth more to him than it is to
them, and he will offer them something in exchange that they
value more. This constant exchanging of things valued less for
things valued more means that things are used by persons who
value them more highly than anyone else. When all goods are
exchanged until that point is reached, the people as a group receive the greatest possible satisfaction of their wants. This, as
Hayek and other market advocates see it, is the genius of markets.

In summary, the requirements for market success are as follows: First, property rights must be clearly defined. Second, exchange must be voluntary and unrestrained. Third, people must
always seek their self-interest by trading wherever advantage can
be found. The pursuit-of-self-interest concept will be explored in
the next chapter. Here the topic is the necessity of clear property
rights.

Concepts and Problems of Property Rights

Although the concept of property ownership is not difficult, its
application can be controversial. For example, it is easy to measure a section of land, plant stakes, and claim ownership. In a
world where the generation of wealth is land-based, the issue of
private property results in minimal complication. However, suppose that, after the land is distributed, one person finds oil under
his property. Assume also that the pool of oil extends under his
neighbor's land. Who owns the oil? The answer isn't easy! Property rights in this case must be defined carefully, and how they
are defined will make a big difference in how and when the oil is

produced. If property rights are not clarified, both land owners will pump as fast as they can to make sure they get their share, and the pumping will continue until the oil is gone. If generalized world-wide, the oil available will be used relatively rapidly and consumed at relatively low prices, unless property rights to the oil can be defined in ways that make it possible for owners to protect their oil from being taken.

This is only one sample of the difficulty of defining property rights. In fact, many property-rights issues today are not simple. Who owns the air space I live in? If I do, I can charge others for smoking or prohibit anyone from polluting my air. If no one owns it, everyone will use it freely and it will become unhealthful, since the prevailing opinion will be, "My tiny contribution to pollution cannot hurt the environment, so I might as well take the convenient way and pollute." In fact, property-rights cases are often ambiguous and difficult to enforce. Copyright laws, patents, water rights, space exploration, radio and television airwaves rules—all are forms of property rights that have varying degrees of clarity and are enforceable to greater and lesser extents.

It is difficult to say exactly how property rights should be assigned. In the example of the car, it is not easy to determine who should own the vehicle if it belongs to no one initially. If the world were beginning today and property rights had to be assigned, there is no consensus in the literature about how rights *should* be distributed.

Rights are finally assigned, however, by whatever governmental group is responsible for their definition. As a rule they reflect the prevailing values present in a society at any given time. Some have suggested that a 100 percent inheritance tax be enacted to prevent concentrations of property rights and so to give each generation a fair start in the economic race. Others support different kinds of tax and transfer programs that distribute resource claims according to some definition of justice. At the very least, it must be recognized that many claims are made on property that is not earned. Thus, values other than productivity become important considerations in distribution of property rights.

Indeed, there is a movement toward increased redefinition of property rights by those who favor particular social outcomes. The freeing of slaves over a century ago was an obvious example of achieving social goals by redefining property rights. Distinctions between property-rights policies and social-planning policies become less clear as society becomes more complex and more sophisticated at shifting property rights. In the United States, the legislative and judicial functions of government constantly define and redefine property rights in an effort to clarify ownership and make the market process of exchange more fair.

Another difficulty with determining property rights is that they can be held as absolute or qualified rights. An absolute right gives a person title to the property in question, the right to use the property as desired and keep what he produces with it, the right to sell the property claim, and the right to destroy the property if he so desires. Many situations exist where some but not all of these attributes are part of the property right. You may have certain rights to a river, but you are limited in what you can do with it. You may own land but are not allowed to build a factory on it. Nearly every right has qualifications, which means that the application of property rights is seldom absolute. The biblical concept of ownership was far from absolute, because only God was the absolute owner. The right to use and keep the output of property was about as far as ownership extended in the Old Testament. The right to sell property more freely seems to be part of the New Testament context.

In summary, property ownership is important not as an absolute value designed to testify to individual autonomy but as a vehicle to serve goals that are important to human well-being. The capitalist view is that the more carefully and completely property rights are spelled out, the better off society will be, assuming that an accepted view of justice guides those who determine what the rights are and that free exchange of those rights is possible.

Challenges to Property Rights

For some Christians the notion of private property seems to violate a sense of justice and the natural order of creation. Those who share that view frequently draw on the writings of earlier Christians who argued for common property as the best way to foster social harmony. One such writer was John Chrysostom, a fourth-century preacher who argued that private property is not the Christian way to organize society:

Mark the wise dispensation of God! That he might put mankind to shame, he has made certain things common, as the sun, air, earth, and water . . . whose benefits are dispensed equally to all as brethren. . . . Observe that concerning things that are common there is no contention, but all is peaceable. . . . But when one attempts to possess himself of anything, to make it his own, then contention is introduced, as if nature herself were indignant, that when God brings us together in every way, we are eager to divide and separate ourselves by appropriating things, and by using those cold words 'mine and thine'. Then there is contention and uneasiness. But where this is not, no strife or contention is bred. This state therefore is rather our inheritance, and more agreeable to nature.[2]

In this example, Chrysostom builds his case against private property on a faulty observation. He picks his examples of common goods from items that were not scarce in his day, and selects scarce goods as evidence that people fight when private goods are allowed. In fact, the conflict occurred because of scarcity, not because of property rights. This mistake is common even in modern analyses of property claims. What Chrysostom did not understand is that if common property becomes scarce, a great deal of hostility can result and the property in question probably will not be put to its best use.

A more helpful Christian perspective on property rights comes from the recognition that property rights and income are very closely related. Wages come from the ownership of labor. Interest is a return on capital. Rent derives from land ownership. Thus income distribution is closely tied to ownership patterns in an economy. Altered distribution patterns can result from changing ownership claims as well as from income transfer programs. Since constant redefinitions of ownership are required in a dynamic system, there may be creative ways that poor people can be helped without the difficulties sometimes associated with income transfer programs. The effort to help employees gain ownership in their company is one example of using claims on property to achieve a redistribution social goal.

---

2. Cited in Martin Hengel, *Property and Riches in the Early Church: Aspects of a Social History of Early Christianity,* trans. John Bowden (Philadelphia: Fortress, 1974), p. 1.

Once property rights are defined in a capitalistic system, the economy proceeds as people pursue their self-interest in the markets where property rights constantly are exchanged. The next chapter explores the nature of this self-interest.

Discussion Questions

1. Do you see voluntary exchange markets as natural developments in the evolution of social organization, or as a construction of thinkers who have had their ideas implemented?
2. Can you develop, from Scripture, the case for individual autonomy and freedom? If so, how? If not, where does the case come from?
3. If the right to own the product of property rather than the property itself (in law, this right is called usufruct) is at the center of biblical property-rights teaching, what implications does that have for modern property-rights arrangements?

9

The Harmony of Self-Interested Behavior:
The Second Pillar

A second topic important to a proper understanding of markets is the way the institutions of a society cope with the people's egocentric nature. At first glance it would seem that if everyone pursued what pleased himself, social harmony would deteriorate. Yet the system of market capitalism argues the opposite, given certain prerequisites in the social order.

The prerequisites have been touched on at various places already, but they can be listed as follows: property rights must be clearly defined and enforceable; society must permit and protect free exchange; a price system must be the dominant guide for resource allocation. In light of these requirements, some observations arise about the nature of self-interest and how it will be expressed. Clearly it must be restrained to some extent or the first two requirements will be threatened. If I think it is in my interest to interfere with your property rights or to coerce you into an exchange you do not want, then something must prevent me from exercising my will over you. In most cases the laws of the land, if they are properly enforced, are sufficient to deter me from infringing on your rights. Thus, if people are law-abiding and pursue their greatest advantage in market exchanges, society will attain

its highest possible level of satisfaction of want. This is the theory
of market capitalism. Since exchanges occur in every area of life,
including the social, political, and religious areas, social harmony
need not be considered a narrow economic term. Both the economics of love and marriage and public-choice theory use market
considerations to analyze very human relationships.

However, social relationships are enormously complex, and
human nature is inclined to find and exploit any loophole in property rights definitions for personal gain. Therefore the idea that
social harmony can be brought about by proper institutional arrangements requires an optimism about social progress that not
everyone shares. In fact, the social harmony of the market system
is little more than a statement that things get done about as well
as they can be expected to get done, given the complexity of the
world. It says almost nothing about how people feel about the
relationships that result from market activity. It does not consider
the plight of those with almost nothing to exchange in the market. It has no way of sorting out what is fair, even though a
perception of fairness is essential for the survival of a social group.
In fact, an entire society could deteriorate and lose its viability
even if it had markets operating efficiently.

In short, long-term social harmony requires a particular kind of
self-interested behavior. Three types of self-interest will be examined in order to understand what is required for market capitalism to survive.

Mandeville and Narrow Self-Interest

The first type of self-interest could be called the narrow view.
According to this view people function in a pain-and-pleasure
framework in which any behavior that brings more pleasure than
pain will be chosen. Life is enjoyed most when a person engages in
activities that produce the greatest net pleasure, so he chooses
those activities to fill the day. Moral constraint, apart from pain
and pleasure, is irrelevant. Thus a person would rob a bank if
there were no chance of being caught and the loot would bring
more pleasure than that available as a reward for the same hours
of honest labor.

This narrow view of self-interest is presupposed in some critiques of capitalism. This is not surprising, because economics is

usually discussed with models that assume that people's preferences are not influenced by others and that people seek to maximize their individual pleasure.

One philosopher who influenced early thought about the
nature of capitalistic self-interest argued that the system would
work for the common good no matter how evil or self-centered an
individual was. Bernard Mandeville, in *Fable of the Bees*, sees
parallels between a beehive and human society.

Thus every Part was full of Vice,
Yet the whole Mass a Paradise: . . .
The Root of Evil Avarice,
That damn'd ill-natur'd baneful Vice,
Was Slave to Prodigality,
That noble Sin; whilst Luxury
Employ'd a Million of the Poor,
And odious Pride a Million more;
Envy it self, and Vanity,
Were Ministers of Industry;
Their darling Folly, Fickleness,
In Diet, Furniture and Dress,
That strange ridic'lous Vice, was made
The very Wheel that turn'd the Trade.
Their Laws and Clothes were equally
Objects of Mutability;
For, what was well done for a time,
In half a Year became a Crime;
Yet while they alter'd thus their Laws,
Still finding and correcting Flaws,
They mended by Inconsistency
Faults, which no Prudence could foresee.[1]

This statement, which suggests that the proper system could turn
evil into benefit, virtually enshrines the *laissez faire* system as
the redeemer of the selfish or evil bent in people. Even the most
heinous person will end up serving the common good.

If capitalist society really depended on this Mandevillian kind
of self-interest, it would deteriorate quickly into a police state or

---

1. Bernard Mandeville, *Fable of the Bees*, ed. F. B. Kaye (Oxford: Clarendon,
1924), pp. 24–25.

anarchy. In reality, capitalism requires something more than this narrow self-interest. Property rights will be impossible to enforce unless people have some respect for the rights of others or an appreciation of a golden-rule notion that limits their individual pursuit of pleasure. One refrains from robbing a bank because of an inner sense that it is wrong to do so, not only because of the fear of being caught. If that moral sense is lacking in a culture, society cannot preserve its people's freedom. The success of the voluntary tax system, the existence of self-service gas pumps, and the fact that cars still have hub caps all testify to the reality of moral restraint in society that supersedes narrow self-interest. The increase in tax fraud and the need for locks of all kinds, however, testify to the decline of the moral fabric of society.

Another way of stating the issue is to say that the preservation of property rights becomes so difficult in a society without a built-in moral restraint that auction, or market, activity ceases to be effective and desirable. Mandeville's belief that the system will neutralize the evil and turn it into good is not a satisfactory explanation of how society can survive and prosper.

Smith and Benign Self-Interest

Adam Smith offered a more plausible explanation of how the pursuit of self-interest could lead toward social harmony. In *The Theory of Moral Sentiments,* Smith developed the idea of *moral sympathy,* which he posited as the key ingredient in successful social organization. This sympathy consists of a person's desire for social approval and, therefore, his willingness to evaluate his behavior from the vantage point of a disinterested third party. This vantage point allows for more objective moral judgments by pushing aside personal bias and greed. True self-interest involves this quality of sympathy and provides a built-in moral dimension that is lacking in Mandevillian narrow self-interest. To Smith, humanity is basically good and the exercise of self-interest is really the practice of behavior approved by impartial moral judgment.

Smith's second far more prominent book is *An Inquiry into the Nature and Causes of the Wealth of Nations.* This massive work describes how the pursuit of self-interest, restrained by moral sympathy and the appropriate institutional framework, works

toward the common good as if an "invisible hand" were guiding
the process. Smith, working in the eighteenth century, wrote of
the entrepreneur,

> By preferring the support of domestic to that of foreign industry, he
> intends only his own security; and by directing that industry in
> such a manner as its produce may be of the greatest value, he
> intends only his own gain, and he is in this, as in many other cases,
> led by an invisible hand to promote an end which was no part of his
> intention. Nor is it always the worse for the society that it was no
> part of it. By pursuing his own interest he frequently promotes that
> of the society more effectually than when he really intends to pro-
> mote it.[2]

For Smith, the "invisible hand" that guided economic activity
toward harmonious ends was helped along by the moral sense
described as "sympathy." In other words, market economies
needed to have a moral or "sympathetic" base before the common
good could be served by the pursuit of individual self-interest. It is
generally believed that this view of benign self-interest, carefully
articulated in the earlier *Theory of Moral Sentiments,* is an important part of *The Wealth of Nations,* even though it is not stated as
clearly in the later work.

Rawls and Justice

Higher levels of morally guided behavior would result from the
application of a Rawlsian analysis of justice. John Rawls has suggested that appropriate moral behavior produces what an unbiased observer would prescribe for a society.

For example, assume that you are about to be born at a randomly selected spot in the world. Would you choose to take your
chances and hope for the slim chance of landing in a first-world
country rather than the more likely probability of a third-world
situation? Or would you prefer to redistribute wealth enough to

---

2. Adam Smith, *An Inquiry into the Nature and Causes of the Wealth of
Nations,* ed. Edwin Cannan, 2 vols. (Chicago: University of Chicago Press,
1976), vol. 1, pp. 477–78.

reduce the probability of starving if you landed in a third-world country? If you would choose the latter, then Rawlsian justice requires that the same judgment be made by a person already born in a desirable location. That person should promote some redistribution of income or wealth in his current situation.

Rawls's "veil of ignorance" is very similar to Smith's sympathy. The pursuit of self-interest must be conditioned by a detached, unbiased moral quality if it is to produce social harmony.[3]

Religious Restraint on Behavior

Most religions of the world have an even higher level of moral restraint governing human behavior because they often assume human depravity. In the Judaic-Christian history, from the sin of Adam and Eve and on through Scripture, there is the idea that human nature will destroy harmony rather than create it unless God redeems people from selfish preoccupations. The Islamic faith also prescribes many social and religious restraints against self-oriented pursuits. Sacrifices, penance, forgiveness, and purification rites are common in most religions as safeguards against destructive self-interested behavior.

Social harmony is generally considered to be possible only if individuals have a religious experience of some kind that focuses their goals on the well-being of others. Only in the service of God and others can one truly increase social harmony. This transcendent self-interest is foolishness to those who are not believers. For this reason, religious people often are not optimistic that the world will progress toward social harmony without a religious experience.

The question that is important here is whether a system like capitalism can flourish without the Christian solution to selfishness. Can the pursuit of self-interest by individuals be self-regulating so that social harmony can prevail?

---

3. It is a bit unusual to relate Rawls's theory of justice to Smith's view of sympathy because Rawls's ideas are not focused toward the harmony of self-interested behavior. His principles protecting liberty for all and the welfare of the least advantaged of a group are concerned with societal justice that would complement and go beyond the scope of this book. For a concise treatment of Rawls's work, read "John Rawls" by Alan Ryan in *The Return of Grand Theory in the Human Sciences,* ed. Quentin Skinner (New York: Cambridge University Press, 1985).

Two comments seem appropriate. First, if the pursuit of self-interest occurs in a context where the individual has power to limit the choices of others, then social harmony is not likely to occur spontaneously. Second, if no such position of power is present, then social harmony can result if a Smithian or Rawlsian moral sense predominates, but not if a Mandevillian approach to self-interested behavior is common.

Some economists have used the term *selfishness* to speak of the Mandevillian view and the term *self-interest* to comment on the Smithian or Rawlsian view of social harmony. The special compassion and love that Christians are to share may help society move from selfish to self-interested behavior and therefore to social viability, but it cannot be expected to dominate social relationships within society at large.

Although this self-interested, rather than selfish, behavior may lead to social harmony, it is not a sufficient condition for that harmony. In order for the economic system to have permanence it must produce conditions that are perceived to be fair by the people of a society. This perception of fairness is far more important than is commonly thought. If people feel that society treats them unfairly, they will resort to narrow self-interest and feel justified in doing so. Decisions to steal will be based on probabilistic cost-benefit analysis, and much of the order of society will disappear. Ultimately, a majority of the public will demand authoritarian control over this kind of behavior, and the glue that holds together a free society will disintegrate. When a nation fails to deal with perceptions of unfairness in its public policy, it jeopardizes its people's freedom. In these matters perceptions are often as important as realities.

In short, the pursuit of self-interest can have positive effects on the social glue of a society if it is guided by a Smithian or, ideally, a Christian moral framework. Behavior guided by narrow self-interest devoid of a moral reference point ultimately will destroy freedom in society. Perceptions of unfairness, when widespread, undermine social solidarity and lead to behavior that can only be contained by an authoritarian police state. Frequent terrorist acts considered just by their perpetrators exemplify this process in action. In the face of such behavior, people willingly give up freedom in airports and public areas to gain safety by means of severe action by authority.

History has not yet proved whether secular societies can maintain a moral framework sufficient to protect a social order governed by self-interest. The final verdict will depend on whether the people of a nation feel they have a fair chance in life. If they believe that they do, then the system will be viewed as legitimate and will endure.

Power and Control in an Economy

Because a morally controlled, powerless self-interest is needed for social harmony in society, it is important to explore a bit further the nature of power and control in a market economy. Governmental authority is one source of control that can create unfairness and perceptions of unfairness. (This issue will be treated in the next chapter.) The other major source of control in society is in the private sector, where concentrations of productive assets can lead to power and influence. We can see how control destroys social solidarity by examining two different situations in economic life.

The first is the farmer who makes his livelihood selling milk to a dairy. His neighbor, who is also a dairy farmer, is a close friend; the two share many things, including tips on how to get more milk from their herds. When one has a misfortune, the other helps. Each pursues his self-interest, but self-interest and close friendship are not mutually exclusive to these farmers, even though they are in the same business. Neither feels that the other has power to manipulate him in a way that will make him worse off.

The second situation is in Detroit, where General Motors and Ford are neighbors. Both are in the same business, but they share a totally different relationship from the farmers. General Motors is secretive with its new inventions, and its personnel rejoice when Ford has a setback. Rivalry and disharmony are more apparent than social solidarity between these two producers. Each believes the other has the power to damage its business.

Why are these two situations so different? The answer lies not in the size or type of business but in the perception that the parties have of each other. The farmers are such small operators in the total milk market that they cannot set their own prices for milk or cow feed. They simply take the prices that the larger market dictates. Since neither farmer's operation will hinder the other's business, they have nothing to lose and everything to gain by pulling for each other. The result is social harmony brought about by a market structure in which the operators cannot influence the market for their benefit and their neighbors' detriment.

The auto industry in Detroit is completely different. There, by changing production levels, General Motors or Ford can influence the prices of cars. When one increases its share of the market, the other usually loses sales. Consequently, an intense rivalry builds as each side jockeys for greater market share. The same situation might exist in a small town where only two auto mechanics or two medical doctors work. The point is that if any producer has a large share of the sales in a market and the entry of new firms is unlikely, then that producer is viewed as having control over others even if it chooses to be generous. The perception can be more important to others' behavior than the reality.

This perception, whether true or not, creates an environment where consumers and laborers feel helpless. Mistrust leads to the formation of organizations with counterveiling power that can increase waste and reduce efficiency. Huge corporate entities are not suspect as much for what they do as for what they represent. In fact, they have generated unprecedented quantities of goods and services at relatively reasonable prices. However, they sometimes are unable to gain consumers' and workers' trust and so rank low in social respect.

When some people appear to have power and control over others, some deterrent must prevent their exercising that power if it is real. If the power of the corporation is not real but merely perceived, then some intangible factor must convince the powerless that they will not be exploited. Whether the power is real or only perceived, the factor that keeps mistrust in check is the recognition that a moral restraint guides the corporation's decision processes. Without this factor in the social consciousness, society cannot thrive in the long run. Paul Heyne, commenting on the problem of inflation, notes, "If people come to believe that they're being defrauded, they will more readily throw off the constraints of ethics and do unto others what they think is being done unto them."[4]

---

4. Paul Heyne, *The Economic Way of Thinking*, 5th ed. (Chicago: Science Research Associates, 1987), p. 354.

In summary, "moral sympathy," "a veil of ignorance," or religious teaching on concern for others must guide the behavior of the participants in the economy if that economy is to be considered fair and therefore viable in the long run. This kind of moral restraint reduces the costs of ensuring free exchange and minimizes the mistrust of power that can threaten a system that includes large, concentrated units of production.

Discussion Questions

1. Is this chapter saying any more than that society will be viable in the long run if people respect each other?
2. Is Christianity required to give society a moral framework, or can humanitarian good will, feelings of solidarity within society, or common-sense wisdom be sufficient to sustain the moral fabric of society?
3. Economists of our day frequently ignore the philosophical and moral dimensions of people's efforts to maximize their pleasure. Why do you suppose this is true? (This is a hard question requiring some understanding of the methods economists use in their work.)

10

Limited Government Activity:
The Third Pillar

T hus far we have explored two important ingredients of a market system: the institution of private property and the pursuit of self-interest as a harmonizing force in society. Neither is a simple concept because both interact with other areas of social organization.

The third key ingredient of market capitalism is the concept of *laissez faire,* or hands off, with respect to the institution of government. This idea that government must have a very limited and clearly specified role on economic activity is not simply based on a dislike or mistrust of public officials or a belief that nonprofit-related activity is inefficient. Rather, it comes out of the eighteenth-century world view that is fundamental to an understanding of market capitalism. During that century the concept of a system took shape in a new way. Isaac Newton discovered that the universe functioned as a giant machine governed by internal forces that continued in endless repetition. Human interference with these forces could only cause problems since collective human choice is not as systematic as the natural order itself.

The disciplines of physics, chemistry, and biology began to perceive the world in very systematic, self-contained fashion. Indeed, creation was viewed as a beautifully designed machine that functioned in a self-perpetuating and organized manner. God was usually praised as an ingenious Creator, but was considered an absentee landlord who did not become involved in the operation of the world. This deistic religious orientation is prominent in the writings of many influential people of this period, often called the Enlightenment.

It is not surprising that the social sciences began to seek answers to social problems in the same manner. Finding systematic patterns of behavior that could be documented and constructed into laws of social behavior became the method of the social scientist as well as of the physical scientist. Economics, more than most social sciences, followed this pattern of understanding how the world works. In the work of Adam Smith and the other classical economists, an interrelated, systematic economic and social order was spelled out. The market-price system, with its great powers of coordinating economic activity, became the economic orthodoxy of the late eighteenth century. Like the internally balanced machine of the physical sciences, economics was thought to be a self-perpetuating system that could not benefit from outside tinkering. No longer were governmental bodies thought capable of improving things with policy interventions. In fact, intervention of almost any kind was thought likely to harm the proper functioning of the market. People acting through government were seen as tinkerers outside the system rather than as part of its internal balance. The natural involvement of people was to be only as individual competitors pursuing their own self-interest. Thus a hands-off policy with respect to government became part of classical economic orthodoxy. Much of this positivistic world view is retained by economists and business people today.

However, few people are anarchists. Most recognize that government is necessary for certain functions, even in a free market environment. Thus, the debate focuses not on whether government is needed but on what kind of governmental involvement is appropriate in a free market system. The following section describes four areas of government involvement often thought appropriate for a free economy.

Rules of the Game

The first and most obvious function of government in economic life is the establishment of the rules of the economic game, or auction. Although much of the environment of the auction is spelled out in the political statement, or constitution, of a culture, some specific economic rules are needed. The political rules involve such things as freedom of speech and assembly, rights of minorities, and rights of the accused. The rules that pertain most directly to economic life are those defining property rights and the exchange process. This requires executive and judicial functions of government. As discussed earlier, the task of defining these rights is complex and somewhat arbitrary. For more conservative economists, the task of assigning property rights is the main economic function of government. If ownership of all resources is properly assigned, then the participants in a system can come to the auctions of the world to exchange their goods, services, and property claims so that efficiency will be maximized.

For example, if a river can take one hundred tons of effluent and still be ecologically safe, the government can declare and auction off one hundred units of polluting rights. Those whose waste is hard to clean up will outbid those who can clean up their effluent more easily. Those who purchase the rights to pollute will be allowed to dump effluent in the river. Efficiency and ecology will be served because the river is still healthy and the amount of effluent it can process comes from polluters who would have the highest cleanup costs. This is true because every potential polluter will bid for the right to pollute up to the point where it is cheaper to clean up its pollution instead. The bidders remaining at the end have still higher alternative cleanup costs.

In this way, virtually everything that is not truly free can be allocated. Governments must still determine how to package the property rights and develop the necessary means to enforce the rights once they are exchanged in the market, but the issue of who owns them becomes a purely economic matter with efficiency, or lowest-cost concerns, the dominant value. The most common alternative method would be to have the government retain ownership of the river and simply decide whom it will allow to pollute or to restrict everyone's pollution no matter what the cost may be to polluters.

In addition to property rights determination, governments must make rules to maintain order in markets. Antitrust rules are designed to prevent producers from joining forces to exert monopoly power against consumers. Civil-rights laws are meant to protect minorities from discrimination in the labor auction. Consumer-protection laws seek to prevent fraud against consumers. Numerous government commissions interpret and enforce an elaborate array of rules designed to make auctions fair and efficient.

Some people view these efforts at regulation as futile attempts subverted by bureaucrats, who tend to seek their own goals of power and income rather than the public good. Thus governmental rule setting that takes the form of coercive regulation becomes license to establish a massive bureaucracy with goals of its own. If the electorate is unable to express its wishes effectively, and if private and public interests diverge, then this form of rule making will fall short of its intentions and may be counterproductive. People with this view generally oppose government rule making that comes in the form of regulation. The dangers of private monopolies or consumer fraud concern them less than the dangers of government regulatory power. Others argue that an informed electorate with conscientious public servants can establish effective rules that will make economic markets perform as desired.

Stabilization Policy

Most people in capitalistic societies today expect their governments to provide an environment for full employment without inflation. Governments have struggled to achieve this goal since the 1930s with varying degrees of success. The two general tools used to reach the goals are called monetary and fiscal policy.

Regulating the Money Supply

Monetary policy is a simple concept with extremely complex institutional applications. Picture what would happen if someone stuffed one hundred dollars into the pocket of every buyer at a given auction. Unless the goods for sale increased proportionately in volume, buyers would bid prices higher. If money were taken from the bidders, prices would fall. When money is scarce relative to goods and services, its value rises and more goods can be bought with each dollar because prices fall. Conversely, when money is plentiful relative to goods and services, its value falls and less can be bought with it because prices are high. In short, the amount of money in a society has a significant impact on prices and output, and many economists believe it is desirable to keep the money supply at a level that encourages growth but, at the same time, prevents pressure for price changes.

In order to keep track of the money supply, most societies give government control over it, including the power to create and define money and make legal tender laws. In the United States, the Federal Reserve Board (FED) manages the money supply through the banking system.

Whether the FED is capable of regulating the money supply successfully is a question on which much controversy exists. The difficulty becomes apparent when one realizes what the auction bidders might choose to do with the extra one hundred dollars that they have in their pockets. Some may choose to keep a good portion of it as pocket money and not spend as much as others at the auction. Since the extra money in the system will lower interest rates, and therefore the cost of holding money, some may choose to hold additional cash that they otherwise would have invested in interest-earning alternatives. In short, money that is intended to stimulate buying and selling activity, thereby reducing unemployment, will still be idle, simply because people's desires to hold money and expectations about future bargains prevent the monetary policy of the FED from working.

The FED pulls money out of the economy if it fears inflation more than unemployment. Both pumping money in and pulling it out are precarious ventures with uncertain outcomes and long time lags between action and results. Consequently, some believe the effort is not worth trying and may even be counterproductive.

The role of the FED in helping to create the national debt is also part of monetary policy. When the treasury of the government needs to borrow money, it pays whatever interest rate is required to find lenders. This effort to borrow for government projects may cause interest rates to rise, so the FED might simply create the money for the treasury to spend. Interest rates need not go up as much in the short run if this happens, but the treasury can then enter the market for goods and services with the new (inflationary) money and drive up prices by its debt-financed buying.

Because of this temptation to expand the money supply too rapidly, some suggest that, to restrain inflation, a precious metal like gold should back each currency unit. This restraint on inflation would rely on natural forces limiting gold extraction and refining rather than on the ability of people to make sound judgments in the face of short-run political and economic pressures. Unfortunately, adopting the gold standard does not eliminate the human element because people must either fix the rate for which gold and currency exchange or face a market rate that might fluctuate wildly. It is impossible to know in advance whether long-run monetary and economic stability would ever result from a gold standard, but the risks of finding out would be substantial. Despite the controversies over how government should handle monetary policy, there is widespread agreement that government must play some function in promoting a stable currency system.

Fiscal Policy

Fiscal policy is the other major stabilization policy tool. It is concerned with the influence of taxation and government spending on the overall economy. In the past, tax cuts and spending increases were thought to stimulate the economy toward more rapid growth, while tax increases and spending reductions were expected to pull the economy back from inflation. In the 1960s and early 1970s these tools seemed to be effective aids to economic stability. More recently, with increasing sophistication of the citizens, better availability of information, and an inflationary economy that generates certain expectations, the policy tools of the earlier decades seem less helpful. Nevertheless, macroeconomic policy, as stabilization policy is called, continues to be a central governmental function in the economy as it taxes, spends, and alters the money supply. The intricacies of stabilization policy will not be developed in this book. Any text on the principles of macroeconomics dedicates several hundred pages to this task.

Helping Where Markets Have Limitations

A third function of government relates to types of economic activity that the market is not well suited to perform. To understand this problem, it may be helpful to ask why those strongly opposed to government provision of bread seem quite willing to have government provide national defense. The answer becomes clear after examining the different natures of bread and defense. Buyers and sellers of bread can exchange in an auction and the buyer can receive the full benefits of the bread when he eats it. However, suppose that if one person ate bread, everyone in the community were nourished. In this case everyone would benefit from one person's purchase, so everyone would wait for someone else to buy. Consequently, less food would be consumed than the population desired.

Although this example seems absurd, it has many similarities to the provision of national defense. In fact, everyone will benefit if one person successfully installs a defense system for himself. Thus, the market will have only a few bidders and provide only minimal defense, since everyone will hope to have others provide the service free. Seeing this dilemma, citizens join forces and require everyone to pay his share through taxes. In other words, government provides the service so there will be no free riders. Certainly different individuals need different amounts and types of defense, but the political process determines the defense that is provided, not the market economy.

Public Goods and Neighborhood Effects

Economists have a word that describes this situation. They say defense has *externalities,* or *neighborhood effects,* that the market cannot capture. The expression *neighborhood effects* will be used in this book because it describes quite well what is happening in areas where goods or services benefit even those who choose not to purchase them. These goods and services are called *public goods.* Clearly national defense is that kind of service. A pure public good can be provided to additional people in the system at little or no additional cost once it is provided for some. In the case of bread, when a family gets bigger, the amount of bread required for consumption increases because two family members cannot consume the same bread. However, when the population increases it is not necessary to increase defense appreciably because new citizens benefit from the same defense provision that protects previous citizens. This important distinction is overlooked by most people who are inclined to determine what government should provide based on some emotional distrust of its role in the economy.

Although national defense may be the most obvious public good, it is certainly not the only good or service publicly provided. Many could be listed and evaluated for their public goods qualities. Some have qualities that only partially fit the public goods definition, so it is easy to understand why so much public controversy can exist regarding government's role in providing them. One example is illustrated by a controversial case.

Public education has long been provided by governments at the local level. The case has been made that an educated society is more desirable to live in than an illiterate society. When you learn to read, I benefit because you move through checkout lines faster, observe stop signs better, vote more sensibly, and, in general, are more interesting to be around. Yet, if you pay for all your education, I get all those benefits free. True, you can keep some of the benefits to yourself, because you need not share the added income you receive as a result of your reading skills. Still, we have a partial public good, and most western societies have chosen to provide at least some education through the public sector. Some argue that we should simply require everyone to get an education and let private sources provide it. Either way, government intrudes into the market in an effort to remedy the neighborhood effects of education.

The list of similar goods and services is lengthy, and each citizen must judge whether the neighborhood effects of the item are sufficient to merit some kind of government intervention. Other markets where government provision is widely used because of these neighborhood effects in consumption include health care, retirement planning, police and fire protection, and garbage collection. Although there are many different and creative ways of helping the auction process to work, it is clear that the market, by itself, would provide inadequate amounts of these items.

This extended discussion of public goods is only the beginning of a complete look at circumstances where the market cannot function properly by itself. Neighborhood effects exist not only in the consumption of certain items but also in the production of some goods and services. The auction process may well be much more distorted in how it generates cost information for producers than most people realize. The fact that the degradation of the earth is progressing rapidly is evidence that economies, including our own, are not counting the full cost of their production processes when they produce. Industrial bidders in the auction for resources may be paying adequately for labor, capital, and some resources, but they are paying far too little for nonrenewable resources and the land, water, and air they use and damage in the production process.

The true cost of producing corn, for instance, includes far more than the cost of the seed, fertilizer, labor, and capital used by the producer. Also included are the eventual effect the fertilizer has on the water supply, the effect of tilling on soil erosion, and any other detrimental neighborhood effects on the environment that occur when corn is grown. These are usually long-term costs that add up without public awareness of the damage. Many are not borne by the producer, and so he brings the corn to the marketplace at a lower price than its true cost. Consumers buy more of the product than they would if the price reflected the higher true cost and, in effect, the market fails to generate the information required for the best resource allocation. In fact it is ludicrous to expect producers to seek these long-term hidden costs and pay the expenses needed to prevent the problem if public ignorance and lack of action permit them to avoid them. Public action to protect the ecological system from destruction seems to be required to bring about the necessary concern for future generations.

If these costs were trivial, as many with a strong pro-growth ethic argue, resulting market misallocation would be small. Unfortunately, there are increasing signs that accumulated damage to the planet may threaten long-term survival for all species, including human life. It is likely that resource exhaustion and the risk of nuclear war will pale as survival issues in comparison to the battle humanity faces against toxic wastes in air, water, and land. Because these problems are not easy for markets to solve, there will be increasing interest in having collective action slow the process of degradation. Therefore it seems prudent to increase rather than decrease efforts directed toward environmental protection.[1]

Information Costs

Incorporating neighborhood effects is not the only difficulty markets have in resource allocation. The costs of acquiring the information needed to make markets work can create difficulties as well. Consider first a market with low information costs.

Picture yourself at a market for a pencil. You examine all the pencils for sale before choosing, but you cannot be sure that the lead is strong or know if the eraser is smudgy. You simply buy one and take your chances. If the lead breaks easily, you will never buy that brand again. Chances are the maker will be out of business soon, because others will do the same as you. The cost of that information is the inconvenience of a poor pencil for a few days. Because the cost is so low, it is unlikely that anyone will set up a professional pencil-testing company and sell information on pencils. If someone does, his customers will be able to share the information with friends without losing it themselves. His firm will fail since so many will receive its service for free.

If no pencil-testing firm exists, should the government regulate pencil producers and force them to use nonsmudgy erasers and strong lead? Regulators could inspect every pencil to ensure that you would have a better chance of avoiding a bad pencil. The criterion is whether the risk of getting a bad pencil is less bothersome than the taxes for the regulator's salary and the hassles of having regulators poking around pencil factories. Probably no one would prefer the regulator, especially if other pencil producers observed the fate of the bad producer and decided, for their own survival, to make only good pencils. In other words, for pencils the information costs of government regulation are greater than the information costs of the market's self-regulation.

---

1. A good place to get a perspective on these issues is from the anthology *The Environmental Crisis: The Ethical Dilemma,* ed. Edwin R. Squires (Mancelona, Mich.: AuSable Trails, 1982). This book contains articles by twenty-six Christian academic and policy persons on a variety of issues relating to the environmental concerns of our time.

But suppose you need a person to remove your appendix. The cost of identifying bad doctors is much higher than that of identifying bad pencils. Although many people would be willing to pay a firm to evaluate doctors, the resulting information could be jointly consumed so that the firm might not be profitable. Also, if people must die for bad doctors to be put out of business, the cost of regulating appears less objectionable. Thus, society usually requires doctors to be licensed.

Between these extremes are lawyers, mechanics, and barbers, who all are regulated in some way. Whether they *should* be regulated depends on society's comparison of the costs of information generated by regulators with the costs of letting either market results or private vendors provide the information.

An alternative might be to require the producer of a good or service to be totally responsible for any damage done by his output. Fearing liability claims, doctors will not perform work without proper expertise and airlines will carefully train and regulate their own pilots. They probably will do a better job than a regulator because they know their business better than anyone else. The danger of strict product liability rules, however, is that they inhibit doctors and other producers of goods and services from trying anything innovative. As a consequence, desirable innovation is retarded.

Regulating Natural Monopolies

Another area of market intervention discussed here is regulation of natural monopolies. If a product cannot readily be offered by two or more producers at the same time in the same market, we must choose between having a publicly owned company, a regulated monopoly, or a private monopoly company with power to set prices as it chooses. In the markets for water, electricity, natural gas, and sewage disposal, it is hard to imagine competing companies running lines through your lawn. Because of the obvious infeasibility of competition, it is customary to have only one supplier but to rely on government to regulate prices at the level of normal cost plus a reasonable profit.

Redistribution of Income

The last function of government to be discussed here, and perhaps the most controversial, is income redistribution. The first fact to keep in mind is that government affects income distribution in some way every time it acts, no matter what the issue. Every taxing and spending action redistributes income, as does every regulation or rule of the game. The question is not whether government should redistribute income, but how, how much, and whether and to what extent the effects are predictable.

This discussion will focus on issues that relate to direct, premeditated efforts to help low-income people. Programs like farm price supports, spending on projects that benefit various groups, and tax advantages for special interests all redistribute income, but they often are intended to do other things as well and usually are not designed specifically for the poor. On the other hand, aid to families with dependent children (AFDC), food stamps, and minimum wage laws all are intended to help those with low income.

A vast literature is developing on the appropriate strategy for helping those with low income, and it is necessary to sketch out the range of issues being discussed. One extreme is the view that the best strategy is no financial help at all. Charles Murray, in *Losing Ground,* suggests a program that consists of "scrapping the entire federal welfare and income-support structure for working-aged persons, including AFDC, Medicaid, Food Stamps, Unemployment Insurance, Worker's Compensation, subsidized housing, disability insurance, and the rest."[2] Murray mistakenly mixes welfare and insurance programs when he includes both AFDC and unemployment compensation in his policy recommendations, but his intent is not to punish the poor. He simply believes that those programs have created a group of dependent people without dignity or hope of escape from poverty. He suggests further that adopting his recommendation "would leave the working-aged person with no recourse whatsoever except the job market, family members, friends, and public or private locally funded services."[3] The implication is that these alternatives will result in a better escape from poverty.

---

2. Charles Murray, *Losing Ground: American Social Policy 1950–1980* (New York: Basic Books, 1984), p. 227.

3. Ibid., p. 228.

An alternative view suggests that public assistance has in fact helped poor people to escape from poverty and become productive. Studies at the Institute for Social Research in Michigan have resulted in ten volumes of research on income dynamics that are summarized in *Years of Poverty, Years of Plenty.*[4] According to one of the researchers, this study reveals "a picture of economic mobility and of generally benign welfare programs that differs dramatically from *Losing Ground.*"[5]

The person concerned about poverty is left with enough conflicting views that any world view presently held can fit well with someone's interpretation of the data. Yet few who come in contact with poverty would support the austere measures suggested by Murray. Although this function of government is controversial it is sufficient to recognize that government has some responsibility in addressing the problem of poverty because of the complex causes and social ramifications that are involved, and because we live in a humane society where people in trouble are a group concern for both pragmatic and moral reasons.

Practical Concerns

The pragmatic justification for income redistribution rests on the fact that people find it costly to live in a society that has no structured means of providing income transfers to the poor. In countries where beggars line the streets, many people would rather pay a tax than face the constant decisions of whom to support and how much to give.

It is admittedly difficult for a government to sort out the deserving poor from those who take advantage of the system, but it is nearly impossible for the individual to make those decisions without investing a great deal of time in the effort to help. The large numbers of families below the poverty line make it difficult for an individual to know where to begin in the income-support process. The cost of an individual search to find out who is needy becomes prohibitive.

---

4. Greg J. Duncan et al., *Years of Poverty, Years of Plenty: The Changing Economic Fortunes of American Workers and Families* (Ann Arbor: Institute for Social Research, 1984).

5. Richard D. Coe and Greg J. Duncan, "Welfare: Promoting Poverty or Progress?" *The Wall Street Journal,* May 15, 1985.

The problem of neighborhood effects also enters if private charity is the sole means of helping the poor. If you give to the poor, I benefit from your generosity without paying because they no longer beg on my doorstep. Consequently, I wait for you to give and you wait for me to give, and ultimately income redistribution comes only from those with the most sensitive conscience. Because this kind of transfer does not seem fair under common-sense scrutiny, society agrees to a general taxation with a more centralized distribution system. For the most part, some waste is tolerated until ways of identifying and eliminating it are found. In short, it is doubtful that private charity can be an adequate and fair way of solving the dilemma of the poor in our society.

Moral Concerns

The moral problem of income redistribution at the government level has at least two dimensions. First, to require someone to be self-supporting implies that the means for self-support is present. For many the best job they can find brings less income than will support a family at even a very low standard of living.

A small exercise should prove this point. Assume your best job opportunity pays four dollars per hour for a forty-hour week. Assume also that all government funds are cut off and health care must be part of your budget or paid for by the employer. Next, work up a budget for yourself as a city dweller earning take-home pay of six hundred dollars per month. If you have limited education and skills for advancement, what kind of a living will you be able to afford? If you are willing to work hard but have no better job to help you improve your lot, then the demand of society for self-sufficiency becomes punitive and the moral issue of requiring the improbable cannot be escaped.

The second dimension of moral concern enters when it is recognized that economic well-being is more a function of relative than of absolute income standing. Those in the middle- and upper-income classes set the standard for success in a culture, and that standard is constantly held before everyone by the communication channels in society. Falling below the standard is depressing for most, but having no hope of attaining a level even close to it brings despair and saps the incentive to keep trying. Stories of people who have gone from rags to riches only increase the despair, since they only make the standard seem appropriate. The miracle is that upward mobility occurs as much as it does, but the data show that the upward mobility usually is not sufficient for the poor to do much better than move to income levels just above poverty standards.

The moral implications of this problem should be clear. Those who have been able to achieve the standard through various combinations of privilege, hard work, and inheritance have a responsibility to those who are unable to reach the minimal standard. This moral sense of fairness underlies much of the social policy of the last thirty years. Present attempts to eliminate this sense of moral responsibility of the successful by emphasizing the ease of upward mobility for the poor are increasingly cruel because the road to success is becoming more and more technical and skill oriented.

To summarize this point, a legitimate function of government is to put in place policies that redistribute income in ways that bring dignity and meaning to life. Where efforts fail, new ones must be found, because private charity is not a viable systematic answer.

This entire chapter has attempted to illustrate how collective action is necessary in a free society. Government is not an enemy of the marketplace but a complementary part of the whole of society. It defines the rules of the system, it operates stabilization policy, it helps to correct market allocation difficulties when public goods and natural monopoly conditions exist, and it redistributes income in a manner that is practically and morally acceptable.

Government Imperfection and the Theory of Public Choice

So far in this chapter we have focused on market imperfections, suggesting that some collective action may improve the situation. It has been implied that collective action can be expected to do the job effectively at minimal cost. This may be far from the truth. In recent years those who question the ability of government to be effective have had a strong influence on economic thinking. An entire area of study called the theory of public choice has developed, and a Nobel prize in economics has been granted for work in this area.

A brief sketch of the theory of public choice might be helpful. First, it assumes that people in the public sector exercise the same self-interest that private citizens exhibit. The public interest is, at best, only a secondary concern for those employed by the government. Second, since policy makers in a democratic government are usually elected to their jobs, they must behave in a way that will insure re-election. The interplay between elected officials and their constituency, by its very nature, caters to special-interest concerns rather than the general welfare of the population. An example will illustrate this problem, which sometimes is called rational voter ignorance.

Suppose you are part of a labor group that is being hurt by the import of shoes from Hong Kong. If you lose your job due to the imports, it may cost you twenty thousand dollars. This is enormous motivation for you to pressure your representatives for import restrictions. You will be willing to donate to the election campaigns of those who vote to protect domestic shoes, and you will be inclined to argue your case publicly wherever possible. Those in your situation may be few in number compared to the population at large, but you are well organized, highly motivated, and taught to use the political process.

Opposite you are consumers who will have to pay more for their shoes if tariffs pass. Perhaps shoes will go up fifty cents per pair. Even if the consumers knew the true cost of the tariff per pair of shoes, they would think it worth little to fight the legislation. In fact, any who had to spend more than fifty cents would think it not worth the effort. Since the cost of writing and sending a letter is more than fifty cents, elected representatives rarely hear from shoe purchasers. Thus, even if the total cost to consumers far outweighs the incomes saved for shoe workers, the tariff very likely will be passed.

This is an example of inefficient government action, and it explains why the inefficiency occurs. If this case is multiplied by the nearly infinite number of concerns of various groups across the country, and then coupled with the fact that legislators might vote for each other's projects in order to gain support for their own, the magnitude of government misallocation of resources can be appreciated.

Other problems also exist when government acts. First, taxes often are unrelated to specific benefits, so that additional projects or favors seem to cost less than they really do. Second, people best trained to regulate an activity or industry are usually those who were trained in the industry and therefore have a vested interest in the activity they regulate. Third, federal budgets need not be balanced from year to year, meaning the costs of government are diffused in ways that are hard to identify.

Fourth, in stabilization policy, effects may be other than intended because of people's responses to specific policies. For example, if the population expects an effort to expand the economy through increased money supply, then it is likely that prices will rise rapidly as people protect themselves from the coming devaluation of their money by accelerating their buying. An illustration of this could be an auction where people believe prices are going to increase soon. Hoping to beat the price increases, they all bid quickly, causing prices to rise faster than they otherwise might.

Public choice theory has its more complicated side, with various voting models and behavioral assumptions, but its message is that government, just like markets, has imperfections. When a market is inadequate, we are forced to choose between two inefficient alternatives: living with the market failure or accepting the government solution. The choice an individual prefers often depends on the philosophical perspective from which he views the alternatives and on how he perceives the costs and benefits of his choice. There is no bureaucratic god with perfect data and a completely unbiased perspective.

The Christian and Government Intervention

Very little has been said in this chapter about a Christian view of government activity in the economy. In fact, believers have taken several approaches. First, there is what might be called the strict constructionist view. This view holds that the Bible is a guidebook for policy and therefore government should not be involved in any activity unless a specific teaching is given in Scripture regarding a particular role of government. Typically this position sees a very limited role for government, even to the point of limiting tax collections to 10 percent of income because of the tithing principle.

A second view regards the teaching in Romans 13:4 as endorsing policies that might be construed as for the good of the people. This provides a great deal of opportunity for the government to engage in activities that relate to the four functions described above. Government, in this view, is not an evil force to be feared and distrusted but a friend of the law-abiding. If this view was taught by the apostle Paul under Roman rule, it is argued that the same ideas today would be even more applicable.

A third view attempts to balance the second view with the teaching in Matthew 4, which says that Jesus was tempted by the devil, who claimed to have control over the political powers of the world. This view recognizes the need for government policy to relate to the four functions discussed above, but it also is aware of the dangers of power and the tendency for corruption inherent in government. The functions most dangerous and difficult to control relate to the military and national security, where civilian control and public disclosure are the most difficult to achieve. This view is suggested as most characteristic of the two-kingdom view of the world described earlier in this book. Government is a necessary and potentially good institution for the organization of the secular world, but ultimately it does not have final authority over the believer, who is a citizen in the kingdom of God first. In short, according to this view, government does have an important function to play in society, but it must constantly be challenged to do good and not evil to those over whom it exerts authority.

Discussion Questions

1. Why do conservative Christians often support more government in the military area and less in the social area, while liberal Christians often do the reverse?
2. Your answer to question 1 will likely be different depending upon which group you are more closely identified with.

What does this say about right and wrong in the area of government involvement?

3. Is the critique of private charity accurate in your mind? What do you believe is the motivation for people to give to charity?
4. Luke 4:6 and Romans 13:4 give opposite views of the source of government authority. Can you reconcile these views by referring to material from this chapter?
5. What are some examples of partially public and partially private goods other than those given in the text? Try to rank them according to their "public-ness."
6. In what ways do you plan for the future? Are you as careful about the environment as you are about your retirement fund?

11

From Models to Reality

The discussion of markets has focused on some of the important concepts that make markets work. Clearly defined property rights, the pursuit of self-interest without power, and the limited but helping hand of government have been presented as important requirements for market capitalism to be successful. So far the market environment has been presented as a simple auction setting with bids and offers determining the prices that become the signals for resource flows. This image is obviously not the way a modern market system is structured. This chapter attempts to give a tiny peek into the way decisions are made by both consumers and producers so that the theory already presented might be connected with what one observes in the economy every day.

The simple auction image is replaced by a picture of a large number of wholesale and retail vendors who have stores or catalogs as outlets for goods and services. Each vendor has an inventory of goods that might last from a few days for perishable foods to several months for auto manufacturers. Prices are determined periodically and then held constant for a while as a matter of convenience. In some markets, like the labor market, prices do not decline easily, so lay-offs rather than falling prices resolve surpluses in the short run. In general, prices respond much more slowly to surpluses and shortages than an auction image would imply. Nevertheless, over time and through discounts, coupons, sales, quality changes, or rebates, prices fall when inventories climb above desired levels. Likewise, when sales exceed production and inventories shrink, prices rise through quality changes or hidden extra charges.

An area of economic theory called industrial organization studies the ways in which different market structures lead to different
pricing strategies. Industries with only a few large producers do
not experience price changes as quickly as industries like farming, where many producers exist, but even in international markets like oil, where large firms or cartels try to manipulate supply
to gain a price advantage, prices ultimately will be governed by
surpluses and shortages in the market. Thus the very high price
of oil in 1974, which resulted from a contrived shortage, led to an
oil glut by the mid-1980s as new production and price-induced
conservation took place. The turnabout took years, but market
forces finally led to price changes, as the auction model predicted.

Cost-Benefit Analysis

The part of economic reality that must be considered next is the
process by which producers and consumers make decisions in the
market. These considerations are usually labeled *microeconomic
analysis* because they deal with the smaller components of the
market rather than the larger, aggregate components of inflation,
employment, and growth. Essentially the process by which people
make decisions could be labeled cost-benefit analysis or profit
analysis. Because these labels immediately conjure up the concern that economists are basically number-oriented materialists
with concern only for a cold, numerical bottom line, or monetary
profit, it would be helpful to illustrate why cost-benefit analysis is
merely a structured way of explaining what everyone does in all of
life's decisions. When one decides when to get up in the morning
or what sermon to preach or whether to walk on the sidewalk or
grass, he is engaging in unconscious cost-benefit analysis and
coming up with a bottom line.

To illustrate more clearly, take the situation of Bill, who has the
option of walking on a sidewalk that is not the most direct route to
his destination. Consciously or unconsciously, he has listed the
costs and benefits of staying on the sidewalk. The benefits are that
he saves the grass, people respect him more, and he has less
chance of getting his shoes dirty. But the costs are that he will not
get to the destination as quickly and he will lose the aesthetically
pleasing sense of a stroll through the soft grass. This list of benefits and costs is not exhaustive, but it is sufficient for purposes of

illustration. The question is, What is his decision or bottom line? Non-economists will argue vehemently that quantitative values cannot be put on the considerations mentioned. Some will even object to a priority ranking of the issues as if that somehow tries to make the intangible things of life coldly tangible. Economists, however, will insist that the mind is actually doing a careful calculation even if it is basically an unconscious process. In most cases social pressure and a respect for nature and the beauty of grass outweigh the desire to arrive quickly at the destination. Therefore Bill stays on the sidewalk. However, if his son has fallen off a skateboard at the other end of the sidewalk and appears to be hurt, he quickly revalues the calculations and ranks speed of arrival much higher and public pressure much lower. In fact, public pressure may now be a good in the good-bad analysis.

Economists call the goods of any such calculations benefits and the bads, costs. Thus they label the process cost-benefit analysis. However, they do not limit costs to easily measurable concerns. That is why, for example, they are careful to include neighborhood effects like pollution in the full cost of producing a product, even though pollution costs can never be measured precisely. In many instances these costs must have some estimated value applied because there is no mind doing the work unconsciously. No super-mind can unconsciously sense when a nuclear power plant is more costly than beneficial. Consequently, economists are called in to do the best cost-benefit analysis they can. Sometimes they assign the wrong values to some intangible bads, but their best effort is better than no effort at all.

Many of the issues that concern economists relate to the task of decision making in a business environment where specific numbers are generated from market prices. A business person looks at his revenues from selling and his costs of producing. They become his benefits and costs and the difference between them is his *profit* or *bottom line*. His analysis is similar to the person on the sidewalk in that he has benefits, costs, and a bottom line. The reason some people criticize the business person in this process is that he usually will not count the neighborhood effects of production (e.g., pollution) as costs unless society forces him to do so. However, an individual does much the same thing if she is more likely to walk on the grass when no one is around than when people might see her.

Thus, the most important concepts in consumer and producer economics are: first, understanding the tangible and intangible nature of costs and benefits; second, understanding which costs and benefits apply to a given decision. The first concept has already been discussed but little has been said about separating out the costs and benefits that apply to a specific decision. Using cost as an example, this problem boils down to determining which costs must be absorbed no matter what, and which relate only to the decision to be made. For example, *Consumer Reports* might say that it costs twenty-five cents per mile to drive your car. If you use that figure to decide whether to drive home rather than fly, you will be making a mistake. The figure includes insurance, license, and a bit of depreciation that will occur whether you drive or fly. Therefore your added, or marginal, expense for driving may be only eighteen cents per mile, and your decision should be made using that figure.

Marginal Analysis and Profit

In many affairs of life, knowing which costs and benefits are relevant to a given decision is quite complicated but, nevertheless, very important. This kind of thinking applies to the decisions of the producer and consumer (microeconomics), and it also applies to the larger issues of national economic policy (macroeconomics). To think economically means to understand all of the costs and benefits of a situation and to make decisions using only those costs and benefits that are relevant to a particular problem. This skill of relating only to the relevant costs rather than the total costs is called *marginal analysis*. It is not an easy matter to relate correctly to either total or marginal costs, but the better it is done, the better decision making will be.

The concepts discussed in this chapter are important because of how Christian people often view profit. In a business context they often view it with disdain. Yet everyone tries to maximize profit. When someone chooses to take the car to work instead of walking, he does so because he believes his benefits exceed his costs. This profit is considered appropriate even though the road is now more congested for others and there is one less parking space for another employee. Christians not only engage in cost-benefit analysis for profit in all their behavior, but also make better decisions when they understand marginal analysis and put it into practice. Being economic is not only good business; it is also Christian.

Profit plays one other function in life. If profits are particularly high in certain areas, they become a signal to others to join the same activity to share in the benefit. If a particular walking route is unusually convenient and saves substantial time, it will attract many walkers. However, eventually the grass will be worn off, the dirt will become more offensive, and the path will become so crowded that those who receive only a small profit from the path may find it just as profitable to stay on the walk. In the business world, profit serves the same function. High profits eventually attract other producers, who compete away some of the profits. Eventually, only the best producers remain, although the process may take a long time.

Profit and Subjective Valuation

What is profit for one person may not be profit for another. The story does not end with the assertion that sound economic thinking is also good Christian strategy. Although the method of dealing with costs and benefits will be the same for both Christian and non-Christian, the values attached to the costs and benefits of many things will differ. Costs and benefits are not technical abstractions with explicit values agreed on by everyone. In fact, they are subjective evaluations of inputs and outcomes. If the two terms are put into a ratio with benefits in the numerator and costs in the denominator, the result could be called a profit ratio or efficiency rating, but the value of numerator and denominator is always a subjective determination.

What one person calls a profit, another may call a loss. What is efficient for someone may be inefficient for another. An example of this difference occurred some time ago when an Amish farmer asserted that farming with horses was more efficient and profitable than farming with tractors and heavy machinery. The conversation between Mr. Yoder, the Amish farmer, and Mr. Furman, the modern farmer, is instructive:

Mr. Furman: How can your farming be more efficient than mine when you get ten bushels per man hour and I get one hundred?

Mr. Yoder: But I get more bushels per acre than you do, and I use no fossil fuel.

Mr. Furman: The fossil fuel is what makes me profitable. I use an eight-bottom plow which means I can farm more land and produce more output and make more money than you do.

Mr. Yoder: You have more money, which you call profit, but I work all day in the field with my family. I fertilize with manure from the barn, which helps deter soil erosion and means I don't need chemical fertilizer, which eventually seeps into the water supply. My crops are not covered with pesticides, so I avoid the health dangers of those poisons. I wouldn't trade my profit for yours.

Mr. Furman: Oh well, this may be a useless discussion because developers are interested in both our land, and at the price they're paying, neither one of us can afford to stay in farming.

Mr. Yoder: I have been offered far more for my land already than I could ever make in a lifetime farming. But I have no intention of selling, any more than my father had before me. My son will farm this land with his family after I'm gone, because it is a way of life that money cannot replace.

The point of this discussion is not what the facts are, because the facts are meaningless apart from the values attached to them. Clearly, the farmers had different goals in life and therefore different definitions of profit, even though they were both profit maximizers. Each saw cost in a different way. If the cost-benefit ratio of farming is looked at from Mr. Yoder's point of view, his farm is by far the more efficient. However, Mr. Furman has the more efficient farm from his set of values. Neither is right and neither is wrong from an economic point of view. Only the adoption of one value system over the other can resolve the issue—and then only in the minds of those who embrace that value system.

The Need for an Objective Value System

In the same manner, decision making in economic life must be viewed in light of both accurate principles of economic thinking and a value system that is accepted as right. Terms like profit maximizing, efficiency, and stewardship are meaningless apart from value-laden presuppositions. They cannot be viewed as technical or absolute concepts. Because of this it is not possible to evaluate capitalism as one clearly defined package. Rather it is an explanation of how the world works under certain conditions. The method of thinking described in this chapter, combined with the philosophy of social interaction discussed in chapters 8–10, makes up the complex system called market capitalism.

The difference between the secular economic system described in the last four chapters and the kingdom of God described earlier is that the two kingdoms have radically different values. The next chapter explores the ways in which a believer, committed to one value system, can interact with a system that assumes different values. To be Christian is not to reject sound economic ways of thinking but to bring to that thinking process values that build the kingdom of God rather than the kingdom of this world. The next chapter identifies some of the values that might set a Christian apart from the secular system in which we live.

Discussion Questions

1. Is the choice to become Christian a cost-benefit exercise for you? If so, how did you quantify the costs and benefits? If not, how did you choose for or against Christianity?
2. You have been standing in line outside the concert hall for two hours and now the announcement comes that the singing group may be fogged out of your town all night. Should your decision to stay in line or to go home be related to the fact that you already have stood in line for two hours?
3. Give some examples of things that you might consider efficient but that someone else might not. What are the reasons for the differences of opinion?
4. In what sense are marriage and friendship processes of cost-benefit analysis? If they are not, on what basis are friends and spouses chosen?

12

Being in the World
But Not of It

The discussion so far leads inevitably to the timeless dilemma of Christ and culture. In this case, the cultural part of the discussion has been the economic side of life rather than all social institutions, but the issues are no less difficult because only a subset of the cultural milieu is being entertained instead of the whole.

The contrasts between the economics of the community of faith and the secular western world have been discussed in various ways already in this book. When Christian values differ from secular beliefs, the Christian is faced with a dilemma that he cannot avoid. To return to the continuum discussed in the introduction of this book, the modelers, on the left side of the continuum, emphasize areas of separation or nonconformity with secular thought and practice. The infiltrators, on the other extreme, seek to penetrate the social structures to reform them. In between the extremes is a mixture of strategies that combine various characteristics of both.

The Doctrine of Nonconformity

I suggest that mainstream evangelical Christians have enshrined the infiltration strategy as the centerpiece of Christian practice in economic life. The almost forgotten doctrine of nonconformity with the world has nearly disappeared from the rhetoric and is increasingly absent from practice. Christian behavior is not thought to jeopardize profitability as the world defines profit. Economic justice is defined more and more in market terms, and efficiency is defined by society's values for both inputs and outputs. We have bought the structure of capitalism with all its powerful tools and fleshed out the structure with secular content rather than with the radical countercultural message of the gospel.

Both nonconformity and infiltration are relevant at various points in economic experience. Both seek to further the kingdom of God in economic life. However, the modelers often are misunderstood as uninterested in changing societal structures and unwilling to relate meaningfully to secular institutions. On the contrary, nonconformity itself can change people and social structures by presenting workable alternatives. Thus nonconformity to the world does not mean geographic or social isolation unless the secular environment is so hostile to Christian practice that persecution is inevitable.

This doctrine of nonconformity implies that the Christian holds a value system that results in decisions that do not always fit the pattern expected or appreciated by society. In an open, pluralistic society, this fact may not be consequential, because people are willing to allow considerable deviation from the norm. But even in open societies power and influence are acquired more easily by going with the crowd than by taking a countercultural stand.

The Beat of a Different Drummer

There are five areas where a Christian will likely walk to the beat of a different drummer than the one followed by the world. In these areas the believer should be nonconformed to the world and challenged to model a better way.

Restrained Consumption

First, Christians must practice nonconformity in consumption decisions. This was discussed at length earlier but needs to be re-emphasized because the secular world recognizes no such restraint. The notion that some restraint applies and that the decision is not totally an individual one is decidedly counter-cultural. To be nonconformed to the world in economic affairs means that consumption matters.

Ethical Standards

Second, Christians need to be in nonconformity to the world in standards of ethical behavior. Most people have ethical standards that involve compliance with the laws of the land or the regulations of a workplace. The norm is to be honest on tax returns, to fill out truthful time cards, and to pay off one's debts. For whatever reasons, most people, Christian or not, go by established rules that facilitate social and economic activity.

However, Christian behavior requires more than compliance with secular norms. Christians have a higher standard of ethical behavior and a different method of defining appropriate behavior. Some examples of situations faced by Christians in everyday life illustrate this point:

1. I work for a company that transfers me to a division that produces liquor, cigarettes, munitions, or a pure luxury good. Should I find another job?
2. I work for a company that buys another company producing one of the goods mentioned, but I do not need to work in that division. Should I change jobs?
3. As a personnel director I must hire a minority person and turn down a more highly qualified person who is not of a minority because the government mandates that action. Should I comply?
4. Some of my best workers have racist feelings and have told me they will quit if I hire the best applicant in the job pool, who happens to be black. Should I hire the black? Fire the racists? Delay until the black is hired elsewhere?
5. My company has 55 percent of the market share and is the price leader in the industry. Smaller companies are inclined to follow my price. Should I set a price that will maximize my profit even though it brings me a much higher-than-market rate of return? Assume that market entry is impossible due to patent arrangements.

6. If the law allows me to pollute the air and add to the acid rain problem, should I pollute to the limit the law allows to stay competitive?
7. As a worker, should I join a legal strike that is designed to get a wage increase higher than the productivity level?
8. As a worker, should I blow the whistle on another irresponsible employee?
9. As a consumer, should I buy a second home for recreation when others in my community are struggling to have one home because the best jobs they can find pay only fifteen thousand dollars per year?
10. As a producer, am I obligated to pay off the debts that have been legally wiped out due to my involuntary bankruptcy?

This list could go on indefinitely because so many of life's situations are filled with ambiguities that make the practice of personal ethics a difficult matter. The objective here is not to solve specific questions, but to point again to the primary group of believers that God has designed to help deal with these issues.

The community-of-faith focus of ethics is more than a matter of discerning appropriate behavior. When believers practice what they believe, the consequences can hurt. The non-Christian will not always be pleased with what a believer feels is right in a situation. The fellowship of believers must stand ready to share intimately in the hurts that result from radical discipleship. The less tolerant the secular world is of Christian values, the greater will be the need for this ministry of the church.

Stewardship of Creation

Third, Christians must be in nonconformity to the world in the use of creation. The problem of pollution externalities was discussed in chapter 10. Here the concern relates to difficulties that markets can have with allocation over time. The market will bring about a rapid deterioration of the environment if people become very shortsighted or pessimistic about the future. "Eat, drink, and be merry, for tomorrow we die" is an attitude that can easily prevail in an uncertain world. The closer society comes to this view, the more it pollutes and destroys resources that, under other circumstances, it would conserve for future generations. An implicit trust in science to bail society out of all kinds of harmful waste deposits would have the same effect.

Without an appreciation for the sanctity of creation because of the God who created it and a view that a given generation is no more precious to God than succeeding generations, the world will more likely deplete the environment than maintain it. Although some may argue that this deterioration is not occurring, there is increasing evidence that problems are developing in the areas of water, air, and soil preservation. Thus, this third component of a doctrine of nonconformity involves a clear affirmation of God as Creator, Owner, and Sustainer of all resources. This affirmation means that believers will resist efforts to allow the environment to deteriorate from one generation to the next. They may alter life styles that contribute to the destruction of creation or work for policy alternatives that will conserve rather than destroy.

Concern for the Disadvantaged

Fourth, believers will be in nonconformity to the world's standards in their attitude and practice toward the disadvantaged in society. This is true even though society helps those at the bottom of the socio-economic ladder. Society has been willing to help the disadvantaged through aid of all kinds, and the commitment to this idea is strong enough that certain inefficiencies are accepted in the process. Handicapped parking spaces are accepted despite the fact that those spaces are often vacant long after the rest of the parking lot is full because few object to this inefficiency, or most redefine efficiency in ways that allow for this assistance to the handicapped. However, it is one thing to provide assistance to the disadvantaged; it is another to identify with those people and share in their suffering.

Jesus identified with the lowly in special ways, and God chose to relate to the oppressed repeatedly at key points in history.[1] The biblical evidence on this issue should cause believers to examine continually the definition of success that they communicate to successive generations in the church. Terms like success, academic excellence, and social esteem are fleshed out in ways that

---

1. Ronald J. Sider, *Rich Christians in an Age of Hunger* (Downers Grove: Inter-Varsity, 1975), chap. 3.

often exclude, rather than incorporate, those who are disadvantaged and ill-equipped to compete in the marketplace. Those concepts, then, need to be restructured in our thinking to filter out the components that foster attitudes of exclusiveness and elitism.

In short, society will provide impersonal assistance to keep hurting people at subsistence, but Christian people must also identify with the hurts and bring the healing that money cannot provide. The trade-offs made to do this will not be understood by the world; thus a biblically informed identification with the disadvantaged requires breaking out of the mold of the world.

Thinking Globally

Fifth, a Christian is often out of step with her culture in that she thinks globally rather than nationalistically. Thinking globally is a frightening venture because of the diverse cultures and philosophies that we encounter. The further we enlarge our perspective beyond ourselves, our home, our community, our country, and the western world, the more competing ideas challenge our beliefs. For the Christian the task is particularly treacherous since she believes that the Christian way is intended for everyone. This notion can come across as extreme narrow-mindedness, particularly if it is coupled with the idea that the western cultural, social, and economic way of life is superior to other ways.

Fortunately, it appears that the church has had enough experience in other cultures to recognize that the gospel can be both universal and particularized to a wide range of cultural forms. For many Christians the same realization has not reached the economic areas of life. There still exists a deep-seated feeling that the road to a meaningful economic life is paved with western views on individualism, materialism, markets, and economic growth that will finally result in a life style like our own. Although some cultures may benefit from western forms of social organization, to assume that they must become like us is usually counterproductive.

Ironically, the move from a parochial view to a global view need not mean a radical rejection of markets or a move toward primitive living. It will require an effort to learn from and appreciate people with different world views. A person who thinks globally as a Christian will be forced to consider the enormous resource disparities that exist between believers in Haiti and Ethiopia and western Christians. The model developed in chapter 6 is only a starting point in resource use because it does not pursue the global implications that arise from it. The responsibility of western Christians to other believers as well as nonbelievers worldwide will require another book that will not be easy to write.[2] At the very least, it seems apparent that a nationalistic orientation toward international relationships will detract from serious progress in this area. As global citizens, believers will be out of step with secular trends that prioritize interests according to national goals. To think globally without a strong national bias is to be nonconformed to the world's pattern of behavior.

In summary, the five areas mentioned where nonconformity to the world should be practiced include:

1. Consumption standards that are informed by values other than the world's view of the good life
2. A commitment to ethical norms that goes far beyond the legal constraints of society, and a community-of-faith-based framework for discerning how those norms should be applied
3. A clear theology of creation and resource ownership that protects creation from the egocentric behavior of any given generation
4. Identification with disadvantaged people who are losers in the market activity of life
5. Global thinking that seeks to overcome the divisiveness of nationalism.

The words of Romans 12:2a should ring more loudly than ever in our consciousness: "Do not conform any longer to the pattern of this world, but be transformed by the renewing of your mind." Immediately following this passage, Paul admonishes his readers to reject individualism and to blend their gifts into a community of faith. This message is relevant to Christians today who live in a society that considers individualism a key ingredient of social and economic organization.

---

2. One source that will be helpful in developing a global view is by Carl Kreider, *The Rich and the Poor: A Christian Perspective on Global Economics* (Scottdale, Penn.: Herald, 1987).

Costs and Benefits of Nonconformity

Most of the ideas presented in this chapter must be fleshed out and practiced daily in ways that leave a clear witness to the values underlying the action. However, these ideas will not sell well to the non-Christian world that does not share Christian values or has a shortsighted approach to the future. Some call for resource transfers toward the disadvantaged or increased costs of production for those who take them seriously. This does not imply that Christians are less profit conscious or worse off than those who follow the way of the world. Indeed, the opposite is true because of how a believer views costs, benefits, and profits. If profits relate to the difference between benefits and costs, and benefits and costs are subjective, then a practice that is unprofitable by the world's standards can be very profitable for the Christian.

Consider the following example. Mr. Cohen is a paper producer who does not hold to the values described in this chapter. Mr. Franklin, on the other hand, tries to practice those values in his paper-producing business. Mr. Franklin has higher labor costs because he has given jobs to people who couldn't find work and he pays them a living wage even though he could pay only minimum wage. He installs smokestack scrubbers to reduce emissions, even though the law allows far more pollution. He donates considerable computer paper to church organizations and several foreign-mission boards. Mr. Cohen does none of these things. Therefore, he has higher revenue and lower costs. Will Mr. Franklin go out of business? Perhaps, but if he counts the cleaner air in the community as a positive return, if he gains deep satisfaction from helping the less employable people, and if his contributions to worthy causes bring joy to his life, then his benefits may be enormous relative to his costs even though he has less money to live on than Mr. Cohen.

This simple story may be misleading at some points. Mr. Franklin may need to raise capital for his business in markets that insist on a monetary rate of return as high as Mr. Cohen's. Also, the higher costs of production may exceed the revenue brought in from the sale of paper. In this case Mr. Franklin could not pay his suppliers and he would lose his business. In general, competitive markets will not allow for much higher prices to support one firm's higher-than-average wage structure or antipollution equipment beyond what the law requires. Mr. Franklin cannot live on the intangible profits of satisfaction and joy. What should he do?

Several answers might be offered. First, Mr. Franklin's life style will be more closely related to the expectations of his church fellowship than to Mr. Cohen's. This may provide some slack in the company budget that he could use for higher wages, more antipollution equipment, or paper donations. Second, his church body might wish to lobby the appropriate legislature to establish antipollution laws or property-rights arrangements that will keep the air healthy. If everyone must comply, there is no competitive disadvantage for Mr. Franklin and the goal of clean air is reached. In the same way, public policy might provide assistance to the low-wage earner through job-related benefits that would eliminate Mr. Franklin's high payroll problem.

Third, a program of capital funding might be set up for investors who share Mr. Franklin's values. This may mean that a lower monetary rate of return is received, but the satisfaction of being faithful more than offsets the loss. As was mentioned in chapter 6, numerous investment funds exist that have restrictions for moral reasons. When this occurs, people are limiting their investment options, even if the monetary return is reduced.

Being separate from the world is not easy. Jesus recognized this when he taught his disciples to prepare for hardship because of him.

> If the world hates you, keep in mind that it hated me first. If you belonged to the world, it would love you as its own. As it is, you do not belong to the world, but I have chosen you out of the world. That is why the world hates you. Remember the words I spoke to you: "No servant is greater than his master." If they persecuted me, they will persecute you also. If they obeyed my teaching they will obey yours also. They will treat you this way because of my name, for they do not know the One who sent me. [John 15:18–21]

It can be argued that if Jesus were here today he would have a different view of the world because, in the western world, there is more toleration and respect of minority opinion than existed in his time. In one sense this is true, but in another sense the world is less religious and more deceptive than it ever was. Mr. Franklin may face a coercive choice: he must forget his desires to help the poor worker, the air-pollution problem, and the mission board, or go bankrupt. If he is alone in this dilemma he probably will run his business like a secular entrepreneur, because the alternative of bankruptcy will bring even more suffering. Being squeezed into the world's mold is more subtle than most realize, and once one is in that mold it is difficult to recognize what has happened.

The best defense against a sellout to the world is a community of faith that articulates a doctrine of nonconformity to the world and then encourages its members to be faithful even when the costs are high. In fact, as in the case of Mr. Yoder in the previous chapter and the apostle Paul in Philippians 3:7, what the world called costs they called benefits.

Infiltrating the World for the Kingdom of God

If the proper base is secured, then the believer is prepared to enter the world as an agent for change in the structures of society. This goal of penetrating the world for Christ is the motivation for much of contemporary Christian higher education. Graduates who can climb the corporate ladder, teach in the best schools, get elected to key offices, or become the best lawyers are held up as models for the next generation to emulate. There is a belief that this effort will somehow change the social structures for good, or at least moderate the evil that might exist.

This model is not the same as the prophetic voice crying out against evil or injustice. It does not ask believers to challenge the social structures that lead to undesirable outcomes. Rather, it suggests that people permeate those structures and reform them through accepted channels of change. This is a noble undertaking, but it is not as easy as it might appear. Two separate concerns endanger the infiltration model.

1. The compromises required to permeate the institutions of society can lead easily to a sellout that means the message is gone when the position of influence is reached.
2. The message involves a conflict of world views that is difficult to boil down to the daily routine in which people work. It is easy to believe that no specific policy change can make a difference. Paradigm shifts cannot be reduced to any individual action.

The Temptation of Trade-Offs

The first of these concerns is easier to deal with. The world is full of trade-offs. When those trade-offs are considered bad they are labeled compromises.

Perhaps the first thing that a new entry into the infiltrating process realizes is that many people want influence and are willing to put in whatever time it takes to succeed. Thus time becomes the first trade-off. Family, church, and social interaction get short shrift. Since there seems to be no alternative, the trade-off gets rationalized: "It's the quality of time, not the quantity, that really counts." At the professional level, the motivation to put in long hours is not money but desire for the advancement necessary to effect change. Thus there is little sense of guilt in the time trade-off at first—not until one looks back on years of workaholic activity does he start to question whether the trade-off was worth it.

The second trade-off comes when a policy or action requires some bending of an ethical standard. The question now becomes, "Is this where I take my stand, or should I wait until I am in a position to influence the decision strongly?" The easy decision is to wait lest the drive for influence be delayed. When I have power I can make a difference.

A third process that dulls the initial fervor to be an agent for Christian change occurs when one realizes that no one is as big as the organization itself. Each person is in charge of a tiny piece of the action, and no one knows the overall scheme of activity. Everyone follows orders and feels little responsibility for anyone else's task. Things like labor relations, product liability, marketing tactics, customer service, and environmental impacts are all separate departments that no one person can understand. Therefore they cannot be critiqued as a whole or individually by anyone.

Slowly, the reform fervor disappears and the standard of evaluation becomes the only mechanism comprehensive enough to coordinate enormously complex operations: the market. The great impersonal magic of relative prices answers questions that no individual can comprehend. Mr. Franklin's personal and interpersonal concerns are swept away by the harsh broom of competition. The fervor for reform was all a hoax, because no reform was needed—or so it seems.

Table 1   *World View, Culture, and Economic Growth*

1	2	3	4	5
high	mechanistic and	what you do	contractual and	high
*	rational	*	legal	*
*	*	*	*	*
*	*	*	*	*
*	*	*	*	*
low	providential or	who you are	diffuse and	low
	magical		trusting	
GNP	Understanding of how the world works	Basis of identity	Type of interpersonal relationships	Literacy

Clearly this scenario does not apply to everyone. However, it is likely to be more relevant the more motivated one is to be an infiltrator for Christ in the structures of the world. It is hard to climb the ladder to power and influence and then critique the system that made it possible.

The Challenge of Comprehensive Infiltration

The second major difficulty of the infiltration model is that the message Christians bring to society's economic system involves changing ideas as well as behavior. It may be helpful to illustrate the difficulties Christians have with a secular economic growth view of how the world works by using a diagram developed in part from ideas mentioned in Charles Kindleberger's text on economic development (see table 1).[3] Referring to research by Talcott Parsons and M. J. Levy, Kindleberger suggests that economic growth does not occur in just any environment. To be successful it must be accompanied by changes in understanding and skills. Therefore all five columns depicted in table 1 move in the same direction at roughly the same time.

---

3. Charles Kindleberger, *Economic Development,* 3d ed. (New York: McGraw-Hill, 1977), p. 25.

From a Christian point of view, the movement in columns 1 and 5 appears beneficial. But the same movement in columns 2, 3, and 4 is less desirable and may be detrimental. Surely a generalized higher standard of living, within reason, and higher literacy rates are positive features of growth. However, column 2 illustrates how growth and modernization move people away from belief in the supernatural and toward rationalism and mechanism. The Christian view of a transcendent Creator who cares about the finite creation becomes increasingly foreign to the modern growth-oriented world.

Column 3 shows how people see their identity more in terms of what they do than of who they are. In biblical times one was identified by whose son he was or to what family he belonged. Consequently, the family was a much more significant component of one's identity and a much stronger factor conditioning behavior than is true today. Today one's name and family are less important than his occupation, and if a person doesn't have a job he feels a loss of identity. Part of the difficulty many homemakers have is not only the unexciting nature of housework, but also the fact that in the eyes of society it does not count as work. Consequently, the homemaker feels like a nobody in our modern world.

Column 4 illustrates the detachment that occurs between people as society becomes more complex. Instead of friendship and trust acting as the glue holding social interaction together, a contract, courts, and legal proceedings are required as society becomes obsessed with litigation and court rulings.

Taken together, these five categories represent a mixed picture. Economic development is certainly not free in that some significant components of meaningful existence are lost. Much of Scripture was written in a time when the lower end of the continua prevailed, so much of its teaching promotes an awareness of the transcendent and a focus on meaningful family and community relationships. These teachings are not obsolete, because meaning in life is still found in these relationships rather than in the increase in GNP that has become the modern measure of well-being.

It is also important to note that the strongest pull toward ethical and moral behavior comes from belief in God, desire to honor the family name, and ability to trust in others and be held accountable by them. When these factors are weakened, the moral fabric of a civilization begins to deteriorate. Indeed, the price of economic development is higher than is often imagined. But it is impossible to turn the clock back on development. Technology and literacy have brought many good things that never can be undone, and never should be. The task is to restore the desirable qualities of the middle three categories of table 1.

The message of the Christian now becomes clearer, but the agenda for the infiltrator is hardly sharpened because the system that gave him his position of influence detracts from the values he wants to promote. At best, an infiltrator can provide an example of personal integrity and a visible witness to what is really important in life. Only those who are called to faith will really understand the message, and they will understand more readily if they participate in a community of faith that models those values in authentic ways.

To summarize the discussion so far, the case against aggressive infiltration has been made on two grounds. First, personal integrity is often unconsciously compromised, and second, the very values that a Christian seeks to perpetuate are undermined by the process of development to which the infiltrator contributes.

A third caution against the infiltration process is that it leads to a revised Christianity that is more compatible with the secular world view. Daniel Bell, in *The Cultural Contradictions of Capitalism,* discusses how our American culture compartmentalizes areas of life and therefore can live for a time with contradicting values. Some of the contrasts in the political, technoeconomic, and cultural compartments of American life are indicated in table 2. The contradictions among the three areas of life are readily apparent. The group consciousness of political awareness conflicts with the individual and self-oriented focus of the technoeconomic and cultural spheres of life. The technoeconomic and the cultural areas require considerable compartmentalizing of behavior. According to Bell, no overarching framework can make sense out of the confusion and so the democratic capitalist era is in jeopardy.[4]

This thinking can be extended to the area of religion. Living with compartmentalization and contradiction is not easy for the Christian who sees in Scripture the need for consistency, even if

---

4. Daniel Bell, *The Cultural Contradictions of Capitalism* (New York: Basic Books, 1976), p. 176.

Table 2   *Contradictions in Three Areas of American Life*

Political	Technoeconomic	Cultural
A group identity is emphasized	Individual initiative is idealized	Fulfillment of self in literature, drama, and music
Equal rights for all is idealized	Self-maximization leads to public benefit	Relative standards of truth and beauty
Democratic collective action is favored	Thrift and austerity lead to high productivity	No vision of the transcendent
Public virtue and self-sacrifice are honored	Winnings are rewards and losses are punishments	Pleasure and leisure are goals

alienation and hardship result. However, the subtle desire to re-
vise religion to fit the mold of society at convenient points is one of
the devil's favorite ploys. The ardent infiltrator is particularly
susceptible to this temptation. Table 3 illustrates the process by
which Christianity becomes revised so it can fit better the infiltrator's agenda. This look at how society can influence Christianity illustrates another risk of the infiltrator strategy and
suggests a caution.

Thus the case for infiltration in economic life must be qualified
by three concerns: first, risk to personal priorities; second, the way
in which economic growth affects social values of accountability
and identity; and third, the way in which the influences of the
world are likely to influence Christian thinking. Indeed the risks
of infiltration are substantial.

Nevertheless, all of this is not a case against infiltration, but
rather a challenge to faithfulness in that effort. The compromises
that are made and the values that are traded away in the desire to
reform the structures of society should be carefully considered. It
is possible that a more radical countercultural expression of modeling might be more effective in the long run.

Here the modeler and the infiltrator come together and learn
from each other. The infiltrator must realize that he can infiltrate
no further than his Christian values, properly discerned, can take

Table 3 *Societal Influence on Christianity*

Christianity	Revised Christianity
The body-of-believers concept of accountability	The individualized faith notion of personal accountability
(This change was brought on by the technoeconomic influence and eighteenth-century liberal political philosophy.)	
The suffering-servant way of the cross	Easy grace for salvation
(This change is influenced by the cultural expectations.)	
You shall have no idols before me	Have the idols but do not worship them
(The technoeconomic and the cultural values encourage this change in thinking.)	
A brother's-keeper view of social responsibility	A self-sufficiency view of social responsibility
(This view is conditioned by technoeconomic concepts.)	
A deontological approach to ethics and values	A relativistic approach to right and wrong
(This change is conditioned by the cultural area of life.)	

him. The modeler must realize that the dynamics of the community of faith do have appeal to many caught in the secularization of development, if the message can be communicated effectively in the secular culture. In one sense the two functions of Christian witness are complementary, and in another sense they compete. When either function is pushed to its extreme position it competes with the other. For example, the modeler who is isolated from society will not infiltrate at all and may lose all opportunity to witness. Likewise, the infiltrator who sells out to the secular institutions will have no message to preach. Somewhere between the two extremes lies an optimal mix for a given environment. It is the thesis of this book that the present mix in economic life has swung too far toward the infiltrating extreme to the neglect of faithfulness in discipleship and the building of the community of faith.

Summary and Conclusion

This book argues that Christians will fail in their task if they focus too heavily on infiltrating secular structures and neglect the function of modeling what a community of faith ought to be like. God's plan for the world, as shown in Scripture, incorporates caring, love, harmony, and stewardship. These concepts go far beyond efficiency and material well-being. They represent qualities that are part of the counterculture movement that Jesus started. They are embedded in the kingdom of God, which is the divine dream about which Jesus taught and which we are to pursue.

In the economic area, the Christian pursuit of this dream has been limited too often to an acceptance of secular patterns and values. This book calls for a renewed witness by believers in the economic areas of life. This witness will require a more penetrating look at the intensity of community life among believers. In a fragmented and individualistic world, where believers are far from perfect followers of the way, the model presented here may seem impossible if not inappropriate. Yet, Scripture itself comes across that way to us many times in those moments when we are most conditioned by our culture. What is presented here is meant to spur creative discipleship in economic matters.

Discussion Questions

1. List some concrete ways in which you feel the tension between being a modeler and an infiltrator.
2. Work through some of the ten ethical dilemmas listed on pages 147–48. Add your own real-life dilemmas and discuss how a Christian value system will call for a different response from a non-Christian value system.
3. Do you think it is important for theological reasons to be heavily involved in the environmental concerns of our day?
4. Why do you suppose God seemed to be more involved with poor people at keypoints in history than with rich people? Is there any significance in the fact that Jesus was born into such a lowly situation, lived a very simple life, and died with virtually no possessions?

5. What obligation do Christians in developed countries have to believers in poor developing countries of the world? Can the model of chapter 6 be applied globally in some manner?
6. Does Mr. Franklin have an obligation as a Christian to do more in his business than Mr. Cohen is doing in the areas of wages and environmental protection?
7. Do you know Christians in significant places of power and influence who struggle daily with the dangers of infiltrating the world for Christ? If so, invite them to share their feelings with you to see if the problems of infiltration discussed in this chapter are valid.
8. How has economic growth changed the way we think? Are the five trends that occur simultaneously in the growth model on page 156 inevitable, or can some be held back while others move upward?

Glossary

AFDC: aid to families with dependent children; part of the federal government's program for helping low-income families.

Anabaptist: often called the third wing of the Reformation. The term was applied in the 1520s to groups that practiced believers' baptism on those who already were baptized as infants. The label also was applied to many sects that taught strong separation of church and state and the responsibility of all believers to discern biblical direction in community. Today Mennonites, Brethren, and various other evangelical groups claim this heritage as foundational to their world view.

Anti-trust legislation: laws designed to prevent a firm or firms from dominating a market in ways that make the consumer worse off than he would be if many sellers existed in the market. These laws usually restrict the market share of any firm or group of firms in a product area.

Bureaucratic god: an all-knowing, all-wise, benevolent administrator or central planner who can plan an economy to provide the best possible outcomes for the system. Useful as a theoretical construct.

Central planning: the practice of having an administrative person or group decide what to produce, how to produce, and to whom the output goes. Market forces and the freedom of the participants in the economy are secondary to the wishes of the planners.

163

Coercive regulation: government directives to participants in the economy that require specific behavior rather than provide incentive to engage in desired behavior. A law against importing cocaine is an example of this concept; a thousand-dollar-per-ounce tax would be an example of non-coercive regulation.

Competition: a technical term referring to a particular market structure in which many buyers and sellers exist in a given market. No one producer or consumer has power to manipulate price. For example, a producer who tries to raise price above the market rate will sell little if other producers do not increase price also. If other producers were not present the price increase might be wise, but in that case, competition would not be present.

Consumption: using resources that are then not available for any future use. Eating food, attending a concert, burning gasoline for pleasure, and buying jewelry to wear are examples of consumption. Generally those things that make up our standard of living are referred to as consumption goods and services.

Cost-benefit analysis: the process of lining up all costs and all benefits that relate to a decision at hand. Actions with the biggest excess of benefits over costs are selected first in a process, often unconscious, that determines what behavior one undertakes at all points in life. If costs exceed benefits, one rejects that choice. Any assignment of costs and benefits is conditioned by one's background, world view, values, peer group, and heritage; behavior is never autonomously determined.

Countervailing power: the inevitable presence of alternative forces that hold in check groups with power in a society. Labor unions arise to counter management's abuses of power. Producer special-interest groups spring up to check government abuse of power, and consumer special-interest groups form to check both producer and government abuse of power.

Democratic capitalism: a market allocative system that is coupled with a democratic political system to form a social system characterized by political freedom, limited government, and free enterprise. The philosophical orientation of this social order comes primarily from the Enlightenment thinking of the eighteenth century.

Deontological: relating to the branch of ethics that emphasizes moral duty, right action, and rules of conduct rather than a utilitarian relativisitic approach to ethics.

Efficiency: the ratio of the value of an output to the value of the inputs used to generate the output. Any value above zero is efficient unless another way of achieving the same result has a higher efficiency rating. A steam engine may be efficient, but diesel engines are usually used because they are more efficient at doing the same task. Since the ratio has value-laden measures in both the numerator and the denominator, it is impossible to use efficiency as an absolute measure of what should be done.

FED: the Federal Reserve Board in Washington, D.C., which oversees the Federal Reserve Banking System and engages in monetary policy in order to stabilize the economy.

Fiscal policy: the attempts by the legislative and the executive branches of government to maintain full employment and price stability by making adjustments to the federal budget. Changes in taxation policy or government spending patterns influence various sectors of the economy in ways that push the economy forward away from recession or pull it back from inflationary expansion.

Fractional reserve banking: the practice of banking that requires banks to keep on hand as reserves only a percentage of the money that depositors have put in the bank. This gives flexibility to the money supply, as the FED buys and sells bonds in financial markets to influence the reserves that remain in the accounts of commercial banks.

Free market: the environment in which market participants make independent choices about economic matters. The inputs provided and the output demanded result from choice. There must be enough participants in the market to insure that no one has power over anyone else in determining the level of price or the amount to be exchanged. The term is sometimes used as a synonym for democratic capitalism, but it is best used to describe the more narrow economic subset of that larger social system.

Free riders: those who benefit from economic activity without paying for the benefits they receive. This occurs if two people can consume the same thing without depleting its supply. Community mosquito control is an example where free riding would occur if the market alone is used to provide goods and services. Those who hate mosquitos most would pay for the control service; everyone enjoys the benefits. Unless the free riders are taxed to help pay for the service there may be an inadequate level of mosquito control in a community. Each person would wait for someone else to hire the service.

Futures contract: an agreement to sell something in the future at a price agreed upon today. The seller of the futures contract has the security of a fixed price and the buyer has the prospect of a gain should the price of the item rise above the agreed-upon price by the time the exchange occurs.

Hoarding: the practice of putting income into a use that contributes toward neither appropriate consumption for anyone nor an increase in the socially desirable productive capacity of the economy. This is a less likely occurrence today than in the ancient world, but it can take place when a survivalist mentality leads to stockpiling of goods.

Human capital: education or job training that adds value to basic labor. It is analogous to adding a tool to a productive process. The same financial and ethical investment considerations apply to evaluating a possible investment in human capital or physical capital expenditures.

Income redistribution: the shifting of income from one person or group of people to another in ways that change the distribution pattern that would exist if the market distribution alone divided up the pie of production. It has been a goal of capitalist economies to elevate the poor and reduce the economic standing of the rich in ways that appear fair to a majority of the people. Income transfers such as welfare payments and farm subsidies have been used frequently. Property-rights change involving rezoning or employee stock options is another way to work toward the goal.

Interest: the return on an investment that occurs due to time preference, the productivity of capital, risk absorption, and inflation. The first and third of these sources of interest were most relevant for people in biblical times, although rising prices were not foreign to their understanding. Usury is likely a synonym for interest, although some argue that usury in Scripture refers to extorted returns above the normal rate. This interpretation is not accepted in this book.

Investment: an expenditure on a tool that increments production in a later period. Saving in a bank or buying other financial savings instruments pushes the investment choice on to the person who uses the savings by borrowing the money. During a time when savings cannot all be invested by the economy they can become a type of hoarding.

Joint consumption: a situation in which more than one person can consume the same good or service with little or no increase in its cost or depletion of its supply. Roads, defense, and parks are a few examples where joint consumption applies. It is customary for these goods to be provided as public goods if it is costly to charge people individually for their use.

Laissez faire: a term that means a system is self-functioning and needs no outside intervention. A hands-off policy should be followed. The market system is sometimes thought to be this kind of a system and so the government is not supposed to interfere in market activity.

Loanable funds market: a market for savings that can be loaned to those who need loans. The use of this term in chapter 6 relates to whether huge corporate expenditures for acquisitions reduce the funds available for needed investment in new plants and equipment.

Luxury: an expenditure that elevates one above the living standard that the community of faith has discerned to be appropriate for its witness in the community.

Marginal analysis: the process of approaching a decision by considering only those factors that contribute to the issue at hand. For example, your decision whether or not to sell your used car has nothing to do with the fact that you just spent five hundred dollars to repair the transmission but on whether you think the future costs of keeping the car will outweigh the future benefits of having it. The past is not relevant in effective marginal analysis except as it might help to predict the future. Those who do not use careful thinking on the margin will make poorer decisions than those who do.

Market capitalism: a synonym for democratic capitalism.

Monetary policy: the tool of the FED to increase or decrease the money supply as desired for stabilization policy.

Neighborhood effects: the impact that production or consumption has on others who are not part of the economic activity under consideration. For example, pollution from a firm impacts the breathing of many who have no relationship to the company or its product. This impact is really part of the cost of the firm's operation but it is not paid by the company or its customers.

Ownership rights: absolute ownership rights include the deed or title of ownership, the right to use the product of the property, the right to sell the property, and the right to destroy the property. Qualified ownership involves some limitations on one or more of these components. Biblical concepts of ownership emphasize the second of these four rights. The private property concept of capitalism need not have absolute ownership qualities to function adequately.

Positivism: the philosophical view that knowledge is empirical rather than theological and metaphysical. Theory based on observable facts is the proper way of understanding the world and its social as well as physical systems.

Profit: the difference between the benefits and the costs of a cost-benefit calculation. Is usually used for the business firm in its financial accounting; the benefits are revenue and the costs are dollar amounts expended for production. In this book the term means net gains from any decision, including those gains from subjective activity.

Public goods: any good or service that is jointly consumed and has a low marginal cost. A large park in the city can be enjoyed by many at once and the cost of one more person using it is nearly zero. Usually it makes more sense to pay for it with taxes than to fence it off and charge people admission. Thus it is a public good.

Scarcity: a situation in which there is not enough to go around if everything is free. When a price of some kind is paid for a good or service, that is an indication scarcity exists, because decisions about who gets the goods and services have to be made.

Spreading risk: the act of transferring risk to some person or group that is better prepared to absorb a potential loss. Insurance policies of all kinds and the sale of a futures contract are examples of risk spreading.

Steady-state economy: an economy that maintains a constant population and a constant output level; therefore the standard of living remains constant as well. The ideal that things will constantly improve is not part of this orientation. Upward social mobility is not acceptable in this type of world since any advance for one will mean a decline for someone else. Much of the ancient and medieval world had this perspective on life.

Subsistence: a standard of living that allows one to stay alive and reasonably well but not to enjoy more than a basic existence. War, disease, and famine were constant threats that thwarted any progress, so subsistence was considered to be the normal state of affairs.

Tariff: a tax on imported goods or services. It has the effect of raising the price of these items, which gives domestic production an advantage in price or the opportunity to increase price also.

Transfer payments: tax receipts that the government gives to persons who need additional income. Welfare payments, farm subsidies, education grants, and social-security payments are examples.

Suggested Readings

Beckmann, David. *Where Faith and Economics Meet: A Christian Critique.* Minneapolis: Augsburg, 1981.

Beisner, E. Calvin. *Prosperity and Poverty: The Compassionate Use of Resources in a World of Scarcity.* Westchester, Ill.: Crossway, 1988.

Clouse, Robert G., ed. *Wealth and Poverty: Four Christian Views of Economics.* Downers Grove: Inter-Varsity, 1984.

Davis, John Jefferson. *Your Wealth in God's World: Does the Bible Support the Free Market?* Phillipsburg, N.J.: Presbyterian and Reformed, 1984.

Duncan, Greg J., et al. *Years of Poverty, Years of Plenty: The Changing Economic Fortunes of American Workers and Families.* Ann Arbor: Institute for Social Research, 1984.

Ellul, Jacques. *Money and Power.* Translated by LaVonne Neff. Downers Grove: Inter-Varsity, 1984.

Elzinga, Kenneth G. "A Christian View of Economic Order." *Reformed Journal* (October 1981): 13–16.

Finn, Daniel R., and Pemberton L. Prentiss. *Toward a Christian Economic Ethic: Stewardship and Social Power.* Minneapolis: Winston, 1985.

Goudzwaard, Bob. *Capitalism and Progress: A Diagnosis of Western Society.* Translated and edited by Josina Van Nuis Zylstra. Grand Rapids: Eerdmans, 1979.

Griffiths, Brian. *The Creation of Wealth: A Christian Case for Capitalism.* Downers Grove: Inter-Varsity, 1984.

———. *Morality and the Marketplace.* London: Hodder and Stoughton, 1982.

Hengel, Martin. *Property and Riches in the Early Church: Aspects of a Social History of Early Christianity.* Translated by John Bowden. Philadelphia: Fortress, 1974.

Klay, Robin Kendrick. *Counting the Cost: The Economics of Christian Stewardship*. Grand Rapids: Eerdmans, 1986.

Kreider, Carl. *The Christian Enterpreneur*. Scottdale, Penn.: Herald, 1980.

————. *The Rich and the Poor: A Christian Perspective on Global Economics*. Scottdale, Penn.: Herald, 1987.

Nash, Ronald H. *Poverty and Wealth: The Christian Debate Over Capitalism*. Westchester, Ill.: Crossway, 1986.

Novak, Michael. *The Spirit of Democratic Capitalism*. New York: Simon and Schuster, 1982.

Owensby, Walter L. *Economics for Prophets: A Primer on Concepts, Realities, and Values in Our Economic System*. Grand Rapids: Eerdmans, 1988.

Richardson, J. David. "Frontiers in Economics and Christian Scholarship." *Christian Scholar's Review* 17:4 (June 1988).

Schumacher, E. F. *Small Is Beautiful: Economics As If People Mattered*. New York: Harper and Row, 1973.

Sider, Ronald J. *Rich Christians in an Age of Hunger: A Biblical Study*. 2d rev. ed. Downers Grove: Inter-Varsity, 1984.

Sine, Tom. *The Mustard Seed Conspiracy*. Waco: Word, 1981.

Storkey, Alan. *Transforming Economics: A Christian Way to Employment*. London: Third Way Books, 1986.

Tamari, Meir. *With All Your Possessions: Jewish Ethics and Economic Activity*. New York: Free Press, 1987.

Vickers, Douglas. *A Christian Approach to Economics and the Cultural Condition*. Smithtown, N.Y.: Exposition, 1982.

Wogaman, J. Philip. *Economics and Ethics: A Christian Inquiry*. Philadelphia: Fortress, 1986.

Wright, Christopher J. H. *An Eye for an Eye: The Place of Old Testament Ethics Today*. Downers Grove: Inter-Varsity, 1983.

Subject Index

Aid to Families with Dependent Children (AFDC), 130
Alexander, Pat, 55 n. 1
Allocation processes, 22–24
Anarchy, 112
Aristotle, 55
Auction, allocation method, 23, 24, 32, 121, 127

Beisner, E. Calvin, 36 n. 2
Bell, Daniel, 158
Berger, Peter L., 32 n. 3
Boaz, 38, 40
Bonk, Jon, 79 n. 3
Business person, 74
Butler, Eamonn, 102 n. 1

Capitalism: democratic, 20; as solution to economic problems, 16, 144. See also Market capitalism
Capitalist-socialist debate, 33
Carson, D. A., 48
Christians and the disadvantaged, 149–50
Church: basic unit of economic decision, 76–77
Coe, Richard D., 131 n. 5
Commune, 98–100
Community action, examples of, 88–91
Contentment, 66

Cost-benefit analysis, 139–40
"Cream skimming," 35–36

Decision rule, 85–86
Deterrent to power/control, 117
Duncan, Gregory J., 131 nn. 4–5

Economic factors: intangible, 29–30; tangible, 27–29
Education, public, 126
Eggers, Ulrich, 98 n. 1
Ethical standards and Christianity, 147–48
Exchange, 103–4; free, 109

Fairness, perception of, 115
Federal Reserve Board, 123
Fiscal policy, 124
Freedom, 32–33, 115; essential to social organization, 102; varying perceptions of, 31

God, perception of, 120, 157
Government, 120–22, 124, 125, 133; and Bible directives, 135–36; inefficient, 134–35
Group decisions, 47, 75; examples of, 96–97; objections to, 83–86

Hayek, Friedrich A., 102
Heilbroner, Robert L., 30, 56 n. 2

Hengel, Martin, 107
Heyne, Paul, 117
Hoarding, condemned in Bible times,
    62, 65
Hunt, E. K., 58 n. 5

Incentives to production, 24–27
Income discrepancies of Christians,
    78–80
Income distribution, related to
    ownership patterns, 107
Income redistribution, 130–31
Individualism, 29, 151
Infiltrators, 14, 145; difficulties for,
    155–60
Inflation, 123–24
Inheritance tax, 105
Interest, 107
Islam, 114

Jackson, Dave and Neta, 98 n. 1
Jacob, 55
Jesus, 41–42
John Chrysostom, 106–7
Joseph, 59
Jubilee, 36 n. 2

Kindleberger, Charles, 156
Kingdom of God, 42, 144; kingdom
    economics, 99; kingdom of God and
    kingdom of heaven, 43–49;
    kingdom of God and secular
    kingdom, 49
Koinonia, 90
Kreider, Carl, 151 n. 2

Lazarus, 66
Levy, M. J., 156
Lind, Millard, 35
Living standards, decreasing, 19
Lukaszewski, Leon, 82 n. 4

Macroeconomic policy, 124, 141
Mandeville, Bernard, 111–12, 115
Marginal analysis, 141
Market capitalism, 101–2, 110, 144
Market economy, 29
Market success, requirements for, 104

Marx, Karl, 55
Marxism, 26–27
Microeconomic analysis, 139, 141
Modelers, 14, 145, 146, 159, 161
Monetary policy, 122–24
Money: uses of, 67; supply, 123
Moral sympathy, 112–13
Murray, Charles, 130, 131

Nash, Ronald, 26 n. 1
National debt, 123
Need, as measure of allocation, 26
Neighborhood effects, 125, 126, 132,
    140
Newton, Isaac, 119
Nicodemus, 44
Nonconformity, 145–46; in
    consumption decisions, 146–47;
    costs and benefits of, 152–53

Oppression, 32

Parsons, Talcott, 156
Pollution costs, 140
Price system, 109
Private property, 106–7
Production function, 27
Productive capital, 56 n. 3
Productivity, increase, 19
Profit, 141, 146, 152; profit ratio, 142
Property rights, 104–6, 108, 112
Prosperity, in Bible times, 54–55, 57,
    61
Public choice, 134
Public goods, 125, 126

Rational voter ignorance, 134
Rawls, John, 113–15
Reba Place Fellowship, 98–99
Reich, Robert B., 72 n. 1
Rempel, Henry, 72 n. 2
Responsibility: in consumption,
    68–70; hoarding and, 71–73;
    income generation, 67–68; tithing,
    70–71
Rent, 107
Ruth, 38
Ryan, Alan, 114

Saxby, Trevor J., 98 n. 1
Scarcity, 17–18, 107
Self-interest, 115; three types:
   narrow, 110–11; benign, 112–13,
   just, 113–14
Selfishness, 114–15
Sider, Ronald J., 45, 149 n. 1
Smith, Adam, 24 n. 1, 55, 112–13,
   115, 120
Snyder, Howard A., 49
Social harmony, 110, 112
Social sciences, 120
Sower parable, 45
Spontaneous development in social
   order, 103
Squires, Edwin R., 128 n. 1

Tamari, Meir, 40
Tidball, Derek, 41

Unemployment, 123

Viening, Edward, 43 n. 1
Von Mises, Ludwig, 25 n. 1

Wages, 107
Wealth, condemned in Bible times, 61
Western ways and Christian ways,
   150–51

Zacchaeus, 100

Scripture Index

Leviticus

25—36

Deuteronomy

8:12–20—54

Ruth

4:14—38–39

1 Kings

10—54

Matthew

4—136
5:13–14—81
6:33—70
12:28—43
13—45
13:18–23—45
13:24–30—45
13:44–48—46
16:16—48
16:17–19—48
18:15–20—48

19:16–22—84
19:24—61, 66
19:26—61
25:14–30—59

Mark

10:35—39

Luke

4:6—137
12—61
12:13–21—54, 57
12:33—57
16:13—61
16:19–31—66
18:24–25—61
18:27—61
19:1–10—100

John

3:3—44
15:18–21—153
17:11—45
17:14—45
17:16—45

18:36—46

Romans

12:2a—151
12:5—47
12:10–13—47
12:11—85
12:13—85
13:4—136, 137

1 Corinthians

10:17—47
12—75, 87
12:4–7—80
12:12–31—76
13—47, 75, 77, 87

2 Corinthians

9:8—66

Galatians

6:2—85
6:5—85

Ephesians

2:20–22—76
2:22—76, 77
3:10—76–77
4:11–12—76
4:28—54

Philippians

3:7—154

2 Thessalonians

3:10—85

1 Timothy

6:3—65
6:5–8—66
6:17—65
6:17–19—65

2 Timothy

2:22—77
2:23–26—76

1 John

3:17—85